T0312277

Cambridge Elements ☰

Elements in the Philosophy of Biology
edited by
Grant Ramsey
KU Leuven
Michael Ruse
Florida State University

INCLUSIVE FITNESS AND KIN SELECTION

Hannah Rubin
University of Missouri

CAMBRIDGE
UNIVERSITY PRESS

Shaftesbury Road, Cambridge CB2 8EA, United Kingdom

One Liberty Plaza, 20th Floor, New York, NY 10006, USA

477 Williamstown Road, Port Melbourne, VIC 3207, Australia

314–321, 3rd Floor, Plot 3, Splendor Forum, Jasola District Centre,
New Delhi – 110025, India

103 Penang Road, #05–06/07, Visioncrest Commercial, Singapore 238467

Cambridge University Press is part of Cambridge University Press & Assessment,
a department of the University of Cambridge.

We share the University's mission to contribute to society through the pursuit of
education, learning and research at the highest international levels of excellence.

www.cambridge.org
Information on this title: www.cambridge.org/9781009467995

DOI: 10.1017/9781009019644

© Hannah Rubin 2024

This publication is in copyright. Subject to statutory exception and to the provisions
of relevant collective licensing agreements, no reproduction of any part may take
place without the written permission of Cambridge University Press & Assessment.

When citing this work, please include a reference to the DOI 10.1017/9781009019644

First published 2024

A catalogue record for this publication is available from the British Library.

ISBN 978-1-009-46799-5 Hardback
ISBN 978-1-009-01148-8 Paperback
ISSN 2515-1126 (online)
ISSN 2515-1118 (print)

Cambridge University Press & Assessment has no responsibility for the persistence
or accuracy of URLs for external or third-party internet websites referred to in this
publication and does not guarantee that any content on such websites is, or will
remain, accurate or appropriate.

Inclusive Fitness and Kin Selection

Elements in the Philosophy of Biology

DOI: 10.1017/9781009019644
First published online: March 2024

Hannah Rubin
University of Missouri

Author for correspondence: Hannah Rubin, hannahmrubin@gmail.com

Abstract: The biological world is full of phenomena that seem to run counter to Darwin's insight that natural selection can lead to the appearance of design. For instance, why do organisms in some species divide reproductive labor? The existence of nonreproducing organisms in such "eusocial" species looks to be at odds with an evolutionary theory that posits traits exist because they help organisms survive and reproduce. What is the evolutionary advantage of an insect being distasteful to its predators? The distastefulness appears designed to deter predators, but can only affect the predator's actions when the insect is eaten; it is hard to see how such a trait could be passed on. This Element will cover the shared foundations of evolutionary explanations for these and other seemingly puzzling phenomena, focusing on the concepts of inclusive fitness and kin selection.

Keywords: social evolution, inclusive fitness, kin selection, philosophy of biology, evolutionary game theory

© Hannah Rubin 2024

ISBNs: 9781009467995 (HB), 9781009011488 (PB), 9781009019644 (OC)
ISSNs: 2515-1126 (online), 2515-1118 (print)

Contents

1 Introduction

A bird staggers away from its nest, its wings trembling. A hungry predator approaches, spotting the seemingly injured bird, eager for a quick and easy meal. Just as the predator is about to feast, the bird deftly flies away, having successfully lured the predator away from its young – a close escape and a risky gambit on the part of this new parent.

A honey bee worker is out on the hunt for pollen. She flits from flower to flower in search of this protein-rich meal. Having accomplished her task, she returns to the nest with gathered pollen, which will provide sustenance and energy for making and secreting the royal jelly that will feed her mother's larvae. Though she will have no offspring off her own, she continues on, flying back and forth, finding food, providing nourishment for the nest.

An octopus searches in a rock crevice, looking for a meal. Meanwhile, groupers search the seafloor nearby, preparing to signal the octopus should they spot any prey. All is going swimmingly, until suddenly, out of nowhere, the octopus launches out a tentacle and punches the closest grouper in the face. Usually when an octopus punches a fish, it is to knock the fish out of the way and steal some prey. But in this case, it really seems to serve no practical purpose.

A cotton plant grows, stunted, with rough corky streaks on its stem and yellow spots on its leaves. Normally, a hybrid cotton plant like this would be vigorous, out-competing its parent strains. In this case, though, the ck^X allele[1] inherited from the *Gossypium hirsutum* parent has interacted with the ck^Y allele inherited from the *Gossypium barbadense* parent, and the plant grows in such a way that it is inviable. Though this corky cotton plant will have no offspring, its stunted growth ensures it will not take space away from members of the parent species.

In all but one of these examples (can you spot the outlier?), there is some cost to the behavior (in terms of fitness – decreasing survival probability or reproductive output) and some benefit to others (in terms of increasing their survival probability or reproductive output).[2] So, these behaviors are categorized as altruistic, in the biological sense that the organism pays some fitness cost and provides some fitness benefit to another. Note that in calling these behaviors altruistic there is absolutely no suggestion of any morality or even

---

[1] Or more likely *psuedo-allele*, multiple alleles closely linked on a chromosome, that tend to be inherited together (Stephens et al., 1950). See also Maynard Smith (1964) who describes this as an example of kin selection.

[2] All of these examples but one are mentioned by Maynard Smith (1964) in discussing social behaviors. The octopus example (with videos in the supporting information!) is discussed by Sampaio et al. (2021).

any intention on the part of the organism – it is merely a description of behavior that we can categorize as self-sacrificial from a fitness and/or selection point of view. (See Section 2.3.2 for more detail.)

There are many more altruistic behaviors to be found in the social world. Eusociality – a social division of reproductive labor where some organisms reproduce and others do not, like that found in the honey bees described earlier in this section and also ants, wasps, and even naked mole rats – is a classic example of altruistic organisms giving up reproductive opportunities to benefit others. Insects that taste bad do not themselves survive, but they help others of their species avoid predation. A pied flycatcher that helps mob its neighbor's nest to scare off an owl does not increase the safety of its own offspring, but takes a risk to protect its neighbors.[3] And so on. Altruistic behaviors, though pervasive, are particularly puzzling for evolutionary theory and there have been many attempts to explain them. It initially seems it would be evolutionarily disadvantageous to develop these self-sacrificing traits because those with the traits are less well-off due to their sacrifice; they would be less likely to survive and less likely to reproduce.

Spiteful behavior, too, is puzzling for evolutionary theory, though this twisted cousin of altruism[4] has received considerably less attention.[5] Behaviors are categorized as spite when there is some cost to exhibiting the behavior and some cost to those on the receiving end. Again, these costs are in terms of fitness effects, and there is no suggestion of morality or intention on the part of the organism exhibiting the behavior. While the octopus punching a fish may or may not be spite (Sampaio et al. (2021) argue it could be), there are other examples where behavior is generally considered spiteful. For instance, some specific forms of infanticide, where an organisms kills (but does not eat) the off-spring of others, involves costs for both the spiteful and the spited organisms.[6] An animal infected with a transmissible disease may make a costly journey to join a new group or settle in a new area, tending to infect those in this new group/area. And so on.

For both of these categories of behavior – altruism and spite – the organism exhibiting the behavior affects not just its own fitness but the fitness of at least one other organism as well. These behaviors are what are called *social behaviors* (though you might think of spite as antisocial in a way), and there

---

[3] See Krama et al. (2012) for a compelling study on this.

[4] Spite is often referred to as a "dark cousin" to altruism, but there are good reasons to stop calling things "dark" to indicate they are undesirable (Prescod-Weinstein, 2021).

[5] But see, e.g., Jensen (2010), Smead and Forber (2013), Forber and Smead (2014), Ventura (2019), Fulker et al. (2021), and Heydon (2023).

[6] Infanticide can also often be self-interested. See, e.g., Hrdy (1977, 1979).

are specific theoretical and mathematical frameworks in evolutionary biology developed to study their evolution.

There are many other kinds of social behaviors. Whenever there are interactions between organisms where their behavior affects the fitness of other(s), there is social behavior. This includes various types of mutualistic cooperation, where all involved benefit, and selfish behaviors that negatively affect social partner(s) but positively affect the actor. These will be discussed further in Section 2.1. There are also traits that might stretch our normal understanding of the word "behavior" but can still be thought of as social behaviors, such as the sex ratio of an organism's offspring or genomic imprinting, where genes are turned off or on depending on whether they were inherited from the mother or father. These examples will be discussed in Sections 5.1 and 5.2, respectively.

This Element will primarily discuss inclusive fitness and kin selection, which are commonly used in explanations of the evolution of social behavior. Inclusive fitness is a mathematical framework in which we take into account the reproductive success of an organism's social partners – those it interacts with, or affects the fitness of – as well as how (genetically) related they are to their social partners, relative to the rest of the population. Kin selection is a selection process whereby traits are selected (at least in part) due to their fitness effects on genetic relatives. These concepts will be explained in further detail as we go on, as will be contrasting or related concepts and debates over the exact definitions of the terms.

Why do we need these special concepts to talk about the evolution of social behavior? One way to think about it is this: In evolutionary biology, we normally explain the evolution of traits in terms of their fitness in or adaptedness to a particular environment. Inclusive fitness and kin selection are relevant to explanations of social behavior, a specific kind of trait, where the environment we are interested in is not something like a habitat, or a geographical location, but rather the social environment of the organism – the type(s) of organisms it is interacting with.

To contextualize this discussion, a brief history: The general idea that relatedness between organisms, or kinship, can help explain their social behaviors has been part of evolutionary theory at least since Darwin. The idea of "kin selection", or selection of a trait due to benefits falling differentially on relatives, was further developed during the modern synthesis; one often recounts J. B. S. Haldane's famous quip that he would lay down his life for "two brothers or eight cousins."[7]

---

[7] See Birch (2017b) for some history behind this remark.

The notion of inclusive fitness was first introduced decades later by Bill Hamilton (1964) in order to help explain the evolution of social traits, especially traits evolving via kin selection. In calculating inclusive fitness, one looks at the effects organisms have on other organisms' reproductive success, rather than just looking at the organism's own reproductive success. These effects are then weighted by the "relatedness" of the organism to those others whose fitness it affects.

Since its conception, inclusive fitness has been extraordinarily useful in producing new insights. For instance, it has helped to give new, intuitive explanations of a variety of traits, including those referenced above (eusociality, distasteful insects, genomic imprinting, etc.) as well as parental care, microbial cooperation, and many others (Grafen, 1984a, Marshall, 2015, and references therein). One of the most famous results associated with inclusive fitness is Hamilton's rule, which offers a simple way to weigh the costs and benefits of social behaviors to predict whether they will be favored by selection. Inclusive fitness, kin selection, and Hamilton's rule are today foundational concepts in evolutionary biology and have enjoyed widespread applications in such fields as anthropology, economics, philosophy, and more.

However, the history of inclusive fitness and kin selection have also been marred with debate and confusion. For instance, though inclusive fitness and kin selection are different in kind (inclusive fitness is a measure of reproductive success and kin selection is a type of selection process), the two terms have often been used interchangeably, with criticisms of kin selection being leveled against inclusive fitness and vice versa. There are further confusions surrounding answers to various central questions. For example, does kin selection's status as an important evolutionary process depend on the so-called "haplodiploidy hypothesis" (which states that relatedness patterns generated by haplodiploid inheritance systems make it easier for eusociality to evolve)? How do we distinguish kin selection from the (arguably distinct) process of group selection? Is the concept of inclusive fitness mathematically coherent enough to yield useful evolutionary predictions? And, even, how do we define inclusive fitness?

We will tackle these and other questions throughout the Element. We will start with an overview of inclusive fitness (Section 2), then ask why inclusive fitness is useful (Section 3). After that, we will have an overview of kin selection (Section 4) and a discussion of why kin selection is useful (Section 5). The sections on kin selection will still have a lot of talk about fitness concepts and will build on the inclusive fitness sections; discussions of fitness and selection are not completely separate, as we will see in more detail.

Many things will be left out of these discussions, and the focus of this Element will be different to many other introductory books on social behavior. For instance, while we will certainly discuss Hamilton's rule, it will get far less attention here than in many other texts. Additionally, many inclusive fitness theorists prefer statistical methods from quantitative genetics, which were developed to study continuously varying traits, such as height or weight, and which abstract away from many details of the biological system, such as underlying genetics of a trait. Instead, this Element will focus on the framework of evolutionary game theory, which studies behaviors, or "strategies", that result from an evolutionary process (discussed further in Section 2.2). I focus on evolutionary game theory, not because I think this framework is better than the others (though it is my preferred framework), but because I think it lends itself to conceptual clarity on many points and can allow us to see some philosophical debates surrounding social evolution with a new perspective.

The discussion will not be entirely limited to evolutionary game theory; other approaches to studying evolution will be discussed. For those looking for more detail on the quantitative genetics approach, Marshall (2015) provides a good introduction to this approach (with a little game theory, too) and Birch (2017b) provides a more in-depth look at the conceptual foundations of social evolution theory from a philosopher of science's point of view. For those interested in learning more about the mathematical foundations of social evolution, which we will only touch on briefly here, Frank (1998) is a good entry point.

2 What Is Inclusive Fitness?

As mentioned, inclusive fitness is used in explaining the evolution of *social behavior*, where how well an organism does, in terms of its reproductive success, depends on both the trait it has and the traits of its social partners. Inclusive fitness takes into account fitness effects on both the actor (or "focal organism") and social partner(s), but the way it does so can be somewhat complicated. To get an idea of how we are meant to think about inclusive fitness, let's look at how Hamilton introduced the concept:

> Inclusive fitness may be imagined as the personal fitness which an individual actually expresses in its production of adult offspring as it becomes after it has been stripped and augmented in a certain way. It is stripped of all components which can be considered as due to the individual's social environment... This quantity is then augmented by certain fractions of the quantities of harm and benefit which the individual himself causes to the fitness of his neighbours. The fractions in question are simply the coefficients of relationship. (Hamilton, 1964, p. 8)

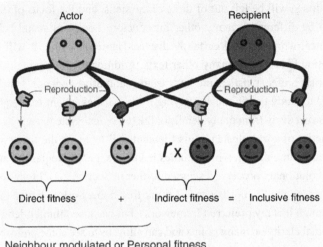

Figure 1 Neighbor-modulated fitness versus inclusive fitness of an actor, from West et al. (2011). Arrows represent reproduction and arms represent "causing" offspring

The smiley faces in Figure 1 should provide a friendly way to understand inclusive fitness in contrast to what is called *neighbor-modulated fitness* or, following the Hamilton quote above, *personal fitness*. Roughly, the neighbor-modulated fitness of an organism is found by adding up the number of offspring that the organism is expected to have. So, the left smiley here is expected to have three offspring, and that is its personal fitness.[8] Inclusive fitness, by contrast, captures the offspring caused by a particular organism, rather than the offspring an organism actually has. The offspring caused by the organism are then weighted according to a "relatedness" parameter, usually denoted r, R, or k, which is a measure of how likely it is that focal organism and its social partner share genetic material. So, the inclusive fitness of the actor (left smiley) is a count of offspring they cause for themselves, plus offspring they cause for the recipient – or social partner (right smiley) – times how related they are to the recipient. This is exactly what we would be left with if we stripped away from the personal fitness of the actor the offspring due to its social environment (i.e., the one caused by the right smiley neighbor), then augmented it by a fraction of the harm/benefit it causes to its neighbors (i.e., $r \times 1$, for the

---

[8] Note: Though this will sometimes coincide with more general conceptions of fitness, for example, fitness as expected number of offspring, the neighbor-modulated fitness concept requires some additional assumptions to be applicable. In particular, we assume that the offspring "caused" by the organism's various social interactions can simply be added up (Marshall, 2015). Nonadditivity will be discussed further in Section 2.3.3.

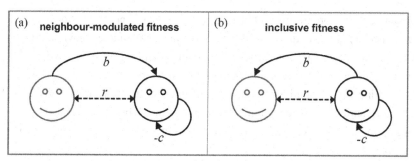

Figure 2 (a) Neighbor-modulated fitness versus; (b) inclusive fitness, from Rodrigues and Gardner (2023). Solid arrows represent fitness effects, and dashed arrows represent relatedness between organisms. Fitness is calculated for the individuals on the right-hand side of each panel

one offspring it helps the right smiley produce). Of course, the "stripping" and "augmenting" procedures get more complicated when interactions are more complicated. These complications will be discussed in Section 2.3.

If this "stripping" and "augmenting" doesn't make things click for you, here's another way to think about the contrast between inclusive and neighbor modulated fitness, visualized by some different smileys in Figure 2. Inclusive fitness is often seen as an "organism-centered" concept of fitness, that is, we look at all the fitness effects caused by a focal organism (in addition to relatedness). In other words, we look at all the outgoing arrows from that organism to other organisms (and itself), where those outgoing arrows capture how the focal organism affects the fitness of the organism they point to. Figure 2(b) shows the arrows originating at the focal organism, on the right. By contrast, neighbor-modulated fitness looks at all the arrows pointing inward toward the organism, capturing all the ways our focal organism is affected by the behavior of itself and others. Figure 2(a) shows these incoming arrows to the focal organism, which is again the smiley on the right, regardless of whether those arrows originated at the focal organism or its social partner(s).

You might think of inclusive fitness, then, as a sort of change or shift of perspective that allows us to view social interactions in a different way. Again, there are some complications with thinking about inclusive fitness in this way, which will be discussed in Section 2.3, but first let's look at how this verbal definition of inclusive fitness is captured mathematically.

2.1 Mathematical Definitions

In setting up these mathematical definitions, let's start simple and build our way up, beginning with a basic observation: In general, a trait will increase in frequency when organisms with that trait have more offspring than the average organism in the population. To determine whether a trait of interest will increase in frequency, we want to calculate how many offspring organisms with that trait will have. So, when thinking about evolutionary change, we are always calculating fitness relative to some trait of interest. Inclusive fitness gives us the information we need by telling us how many offspring are caused by an organism and how likely it is that these offspring are had by an organism with the trait of interest.

Following Figure 1, we might write the equation for inclusive fitness, denoted IF, this way:

$$\text{IF} = \text{direct fitness} + \text{indirect fitness}, \tag{1}$$

where "direct fitness" captures the fitness self-effects (how many offspring the organisms with the trait cause themselves to have), and "indirect fitness" captures the fitness other-effects (how many offspring organisms with the trait cause others to have), weighted by how likely it is those others also have the trait, relative to the rest of the population. These two terms, taken together, tell us how many offspring are produced by organisms with the trait of interest.

We then have to mathematically capture these different types of fitness effects. The simplest way to do this is to assign variable names to the self-effect ($-c$), other-effect (b), and relatedness (r). Inclusive fitness, after reordering terms to get things into the familiar form, is then:

$$\text{IF} = rb - c. \tag{2}$$

Since explanations of social evolution tend to focus on altruistic traits, c and b are often interpreted as "cost" and "benefit", respectively, though there is no limitation in the theory that says the self-effect must be negative or the other-effect positive. In fact, to categorize different social behaviors, people commonly make use of a four-part schema introduced by Hamilton (1964), which distinguishes between positive and negative fitness effects, both for the actor, or focal organism exhibiting the behavior of interest, and the recipient, or social partner interacting with the focal organism. In Table 1, the first cell is mutual benefit ($+,+$), the second is selfishness ($+,-$), the third is altruism ($-,+$), and the fourth is spite ($-,-$). Many times, mutual benefit and altruism are grouped together as "cooperative" or "pro-social".

The formulation of inclusive fitness in Eq. (2) is often associated with Hamilton's rule, according to which a social trait is favored by natural selection when

$$rb - c > 0, \tag{3}$$

Table 1 Four-part schema for categorizing social behavior

		Recipient	
		+	−
Actor	+	Mutual Benefit	Selfishness
	−	Altruism	Spite

where, again, the $-c$ and b terms capture the self-effect and the other-effect for the trait in question, and r relatedness between organisms with the trait and their social partners. Hamilton's rule tells us exactly how the costs and benefits of a social behavior ought to be compared to each other in predicting whether it will be favored by selection. Since relatedness captures how similar the organisms are, relative to the rest of the population, this rule captures the fact that the benefits of altruistic behavior must fall on altruists sufficiently more often than non-altruists for it to outweigh the costs they are incurring. (More on relatedness shortly.)

Of course, we want to do more than just assign variable names. We want a way to talk about these terms as measured experimentally or as captured by a mathematical model, and there are different ways to do this. With apologies for front-loading this Element with mathematical details, we will discuss a couple methods of calculating inclusive fitness now.

One very common way is to look at how an organisms' traits covary with their own fitness and with the fitness of social partners. This approach usually starts with the Price equation, which is a general description of evolutionary change. Let f be the fitness of a trait in the population. Then, the Price equation describes expected evolutionary change in the following way:

$$\dot{E}(p) = Cov(f,p). \tag{4}$$

We often think of p as phenotypic value, capturing some observable feature of the organism, such as its height or its altruistic tendency, although p can actually represent anything a modeler might want to keep track of: phenotypic value, genetic value, frequency of a trait, and so on. $\dot{E}(p)$ is then the change in the average (phenotypic) value in the population. The covariance term, $Cov(f,p)$, measures how fitness changes with differences in phenotype.[9]

---

[9] There is sometimes a second term, $E_f(\dot{p})$, included which measures the fitness-weighted transmission bias, the difference between the phenotypic value of a parent and the average phenotypic value of their offspring. It is often assumed that $E_f(\dot{p}) = 0$, which is described as

Under certain assumptions, which will be described in Section 2.3, we can derive equations for both inclusive fitness and neighbor-modulated fitness from the Price equation. Here is the equation for inclusive fitness:

$$\text{IF} = \beta_{s_{i-i}p} \cdot \frac{Cov(p, g')}{Cov(p, g)} - \beta_{s_{ii}p}. \tag{5}$$

To explain what these terms mean: $\beta_{s_{ii}p}$ is a regression of an organism i's phenotype on its own fitness (i.e., how its behavior affects its reproductive success); $\beta_{s_{i-i}p}$ is a regression of an organism's phenotype on its social partner $-i$'s fitness (i.e., how its behavior affects its social partner's reproductive success); and, finally, $\frac{Cov(p,g')}{Cov(p,g)}$ is our a measure of relatedness, r. This measure of relatedness compares the covariance between a focal organism's phenotype, p, and its social partner's genotype, g', with the covariance between the focal organism's phenotype and its own genotype, g (Orlove and Wood, 1978).[10] It is a measure of the degree to which the focal organism and its social partner are genetically related, or how likely it is that the fitness effects from a trait fall on organisms with the gene(s) encoding for the trait. When we interpret $\beta_{s_{ii}p}$ as a "cost" and $\beta_{s_{i-i}p}$ as a "benefit", we have our inclusive fitness calculation, $\text{IF} = rb - c$.

Later, we will get into more detail on each of these terms – self-effect, other-effect, relatedness – and how to make sense of what they capture. For now, it is important to note (since it is often a cause for confusion) that relatedness is *not* just the probability that the two organisms share the allele (version of a gene) of interest. It is a measure of their genetic similarity relative to the genetic composition of the population as a whole. This matters because in studying altruism, for example, we want to know whether the benefits of altruistic acts fall on altruists sufficiently *more often* than they fall on non-altruists. That is, the benefits must fall on altruists rather than non-altruists with sufficient frequency to give them a reproductive advantage over non-altruists.

As there are many ways to mathematically capture inclusive fitness, this section could go on and on. For the sake of moving along to more philosophical issues, though, I will restrain myself and discuss just one more that will be important in what follows. Rather than using a statistical definition, we might instead use something that is more amenable to the types of models used in evolutionary game theory. Using similar notation as before, when i interacts

---

assuming there is no transmission bias. Assuming that $E_f(p) = 0$ is not exactly the same as assuming there is no transmission bias (van Veelen, 2005), but the details of what exactly it means to assume $E_f(p) = 0$ are not crucial here.

[10] When phenotypes are a linear function of genotypes (i.e., when there's no dominance or gene-environment correlations), relatedness can instead be given in a purely genetic form, as a regression $\frac{Cov(g,g')}{Cov(g,g)}$ (Queller, 1992a).

with other organisms, it affects its own fitness by some amount (s_{ii}) and the fitness of another organism, $-i$, by some amount (s_{i-i}). In this context, these effects are given by the model; they are stipulated, not measured or estimated. Similarly, the probability of interacting with another organism that has the trait of interest, T, depends on whether an organism has T or not (denoted N) in a way defined by the assumptions of the model.

We can then define inclusive fitness as follows:

$$\text{IF} = s_{ii} + [P(T_{-i}|T_i) - P(T_{-i}|N_i)]s_{i-i}. \tag{6}$$

The relatedness between interacting organisms, $r = P(T_{-i}|T_i) - P(T_{-i}|N_i)$, is defined as a difference in conditional probabilities: How likely the focal organism is to interact with another organism that has the trait of interest, given that either it has or does not have the trait itself (Skyrms, 2002, van Veelen, 2009, Okasha and Martens, 2016b, Rubin, 2018). Again, remember that this is a measure of the *differential* likelihood your social partners are like you, that is, compared to the population as a whole. When $s_{ii} = -c$ and $s_{i-i} = b$, inclusive fitness is, as in Eq. (2), $rb - c$.

The various ways to mathematically capture inclusive fitness are not totally disconnected. There are different calculations based off the Price equation that are all interrelated (Marshall, 2015), and the statistical definition in Eq. (5) is equivalent to the game theoretic calculation just discussed in Eq. (6), under certain conditions (Rubin, 2018).[11]

2.2 Social Evolution

To connect this more explicitly to evolutionary game theory, note that the altruistic interactions we have been describing can be captured by one of the most famous games in game theory, the prisoners' dilemma, shown in Table 2.[12] In a game theoretic setup, we view both the actor and recipient as *players* in the game. The actor's strategies – possible social behaviors it might exhibit – are written in the rows, and the social partner's strategies are written in the columns. The payoffs players get for choosing altruism or non-altruism, depending on the trait of their social partner, are summarized in the cells of the tables. Note that I have switched from talking about fitness effects to payoffs, but this is only a difference in terminology between evolutionary theory and decision theory. The payoffs just represent what the decision-maker "cares" about, the

---

[11] For example, when there are a finite number of types under consideration, additive payoffs, and pairwise interactions.

[12] This version of the prisoners' dilemma is also sometimes called a donation game, as the two strategies can be thought of as a choice between donating or not, where what is to be donated has value c to the actor and value b to the recipient.

Table 2 Prisoners' dilemmas. (a) a prisoners' dilemma arising from a generic choice of whether or not to be altruistic, and (b) a prisoners' dilemma with $b = 2$ and $c = 1$.

	Altruist	Not			Altruist	Not
Altruist	$b - c, b - c$	$-c, b$		Altruist	1, 1	$-1, 2$
Not	$b, -c$	0, 0		Not	2, -1	0, 0
	(a)				(b)	

utility they assign to outcomes, which, when talking about evolution of traits, just represents the fitness of the organism. Talking this way seems to require some sort of agential thinking or analogizing – we will return to this topic in Section 3.1.

Classical game theory considers rational actors playing the game and calculating the optimal action. In this game, the rational choice is always to choose *not* to be altruistic: If your social partner is an altruist, you get a payoff of b rather than $b - c$ and if your social partner is not an altruist, you get a payoff of zero rather than $-c$. Switching to the viewpoint of evolutionary game theory, we consider behaviors or strategies as the outcome of an evolutionary process, whether that process is biological or captures some kind of cultural learning. Here, we will focus on biological evolution via natural selection. For discussions of cultural evolution, see, for example, Henrich (2004), Mesoudi et al. (2006), Jablonka and Lamb (2014), as well as Section 5.4 of this Element.

When interactions in a population are random, the evolutionary prediction will be the same as the rational choice for the game: Evolution will lead to a population of non-altruists, just as if the organisms were rational agents choosing their traits in order to maximize their fitness. However, interactions in a population are not always random. There is often *correlation* or *assortment* between types, where organisms are more likely to interact with other organisms of their same type. Altruists are more likely to interact with other altruists and non-altruists are more likely to interact with other non-altruists for a variety of reasons. This could be because of "greenbeard" effects, where altruists have some observable trait allowing them to recognize and preferentially interact with other altruists (Dawkins, 1976), for example, or because organisms interact with their kin who tend to have the same inherited traits as them, and so on. If there is sufficient correlation between types, the population will evolve to become composed entirely of altruists.

Inclusive fitness is one way to mathematically capture the effect of these correlations, as relatedness is a measure of correlation between types,[13] or how likely it is that the focal organism and its social partner share genetic material, relative to the rest of the population. So, the inclusive fitness of an altruist in the prisoner' dilemma in Table 2(a) would be $-c + rb$ because the self-effect is $-c$ and the other-effect is b.

Inclusive fitness can be used with the standard dynamical equations employed by evolutionary game theorists, for example, the replicator dynamics. Under this dynamics, if the fitness of a trait is greater than the average fitness of the population, the frequency of the trait will increase. The traits of interest dictate behavior in some social interaction, so a trait's fitness is determined by how well it does against the other possible traits in the population (in addition to the population composition). If x_t is the frequency of the trait of interest, and $f_t(x)$ its fitness in a population of composition x, the replicator dynamics is governed by the following equation:

$$\dot{x}_t = x_t[f_t(x) - \bar{f}(x)]. \tag{7}$$

We just interpret $f_t(x)$ as inclusive fitness and $\bar{f}(x)$ as the average inclusive fitness in the population, and the replicator dynamics gives the same predictions as if we interpreted fitness as expected number of offspring, or something similar.[14]

2.3 Complications and Provisos

The previous sections give nice, clean definitions of inclusive fitness. As an introduction to the subject, this is a natural way to begin. However, it is not all as simple as it seems. So, here I discuss just a few of many provisos and complications, and how inclusive fitness theorists deal with them.

2.3.1 Background Fitness

The first is quite simple and quick to incorporate: Inclusive fitness, like many other ways of calculating fitness, often includes what's called "background fitness". That is, the fitness effects we have been discussing are those fitness effects that arise due to some trait of interest (namely: whatever trait we are interested in explaining the evolution of). Of course, organisms' lives don't all revolve around one particular trait; they have other stuff going on. Lots of other traits factor in to whether they live or die, reproduce or not. The contribution of these other traits is generally summarized as background fitness, often denoted

---

[13] See, e.g., Marshall (2015), and references therein.
[14] See Rubin (2018) for further discussion.

f_0 or w_0, that is the same for all organisms in the population. Since we are interested how natural selection acts on one particular trait, this allows us to isolate the effects of that trait. The idea is that, while organisms likely have different combinations of other traits and so different fitness due to those other traits, if those other traits are not correlated with our trait of interest we can safely just assign everyone the same background fitness and the analysis can proceed.[15]

2.3.2 What Is a Trait?

Second, we should consider the casual use of the word "trait" to this point. In many nonsocial settings, describing the trait of interest is often easy and unproblematic: an organism's height, or speed, or flower color, or some other such property we can point to. When discussing social behaviors, however, definitions of traits are often more hazy. We have been giving examples of behavior and lumping them under terms "altruism" or "spite", then defining fitness for this "altruism" or "spite". Do we mean that what evolves is some general altruistic tendency that kicks in for all interactions, or a very specific behavior in one instance of an interaction that can be captured by a specific prisoners' dilemma, or something in between, like a strategy for all prisoners' dilemma-type interactions? In some contexts, even in social evolution, this question will not matter too much, for example, simple models in evolutionary game theory. However, it would be good if we generally had an idea of what a "trait" is when talking about the evolution of social behaviors.

People often assume that when we use game theory to capture the social interactions important to fitness, this means we must be thinking of organisms as engaging in, for example, a prisoners' dilemma, with one other organism and then moving on with their lives. This impression does not come from nowhere; we often describe evolutionary games using such phrases as "the payoff an altruist gets when interacting with another altruist" or "the likelihood an altruist interacts with another altruist". And this makes evolutionary game theory seem quite restricted in its range of application. Fortunately, using games to capture social behavior is not quite so restricted. These payoffs do not have to capture fitness effects from only *one* social interaction, they can be the average fitness effects incurred from exhibiting a particular kind of behavior (altruistic or not) in a particular kind of situation (that can be captured by our game or payoff table). Interaction probabilities can be interpreted similarly; not the chance an

---

[15]   This focus on the theoretical construct of background fitness is not to make it sound like there is meanwhile a big empirical problem – you can still talk about background fitness versus fitness effects with respect to empirical observations.

organism runs into an altruist this one time, but instead capturing its tendency to interact with altruists versus non-altruists in these types of situations over its lifetime.

This more liberal interpretation of payoffs and interaction probabilities allows us to say something more plausible about the traits under consideration – we are not restricted to saying that a trait is a particular action an organism takes once in its lifetime, or a strategy employed in a single game. Instead, we might say something like: When we are talking about the evolution of altruism, the trait of interest is a tendency to behave in a particular way in situations captured by a prisoners' dilemma. We still might want to be more explicit about what the "trait" is, though, and there are various ways to spell that out. For instance, an organism might have multiple, very disparate, interactions in its lifetime that could be captured by a prisoners' dilemma and its behavior in one context might bear no relation to its behavior in another. So we might want to place some restrictions and say which prisoners' dilemmas are relevant. Some authors, for instance, talk about "collaborative contexts" or specific tasks that are to be performed (Anderson and Franks, 2001, Anderson and McShea, 2001, Anderson et al., 2001, Calcott, 2008, Birch, 2017b).[16] For example, in certain ant colonies, teams are formed to perform the task of defending against an intruder, where one type of ant pins down the intruder and the other type decapitates it.

Taking a longer view than just a single interaction is also relevant to debates regarding categorizing behaviors as altruistic or not. Many argue that *lifetime fitness*, that is, how a trait affects an organism's reproductive success over their lifetime, should be the relevant consideration for classification (see, e.g. West et al., 2007, Bowles and Gintis, 2011). So, behaviors that temporarily lower fitness but in the end increase overall expected fitness would not count as altruistic. A classic example of this sort of behavior is reciprocal altruism (Trivers, 1971), where an organism will behave altruistically toward another (decreasing fitness in the short term, immediately following that interaction), which leads to more altruistic actions to be directed toward them in the future (for an overall lifetime benefit to fitness). Reciprocal altruism, it is argued, then, is not properly altruism, and these sorts of behaviors are often instead called reciprocity, rather than reciprocal altruism (e.g., in Axelrod and Hamilton, 1981, Trivers, 1985).

---

[16] Birch, for instance, is concerned with classifying particular actions as altruistic, cooperative, and so on. He argues that these classifications depend on what kind of strategy the action is part of, the relevant task, and recent selection history (Birch, 2017b, p.28-34).

Of course, there is more to say about specifying what traits are and how to classify them.[17] Spelling out all the issues involved would take us too far from the main focus of this Element on inclusive fitness and kin selection. Instead, I will just note one more issue when it comes to defining traits in the context of social behavior. Though there many attempts at defining social traits (e.g., altruism, cooperation) based on purely biological criteria, we may never fully remove our intuitions from the mix. Halperin and Levy (2022) make this argument in the context of attempts to classify behaviors as altruistic or not. They argue that our intuitions affect which organism we see as the actor and recipient (i.e., who is performing the action?) in any given social interaction, which means it is impossible to distinguish, for example, altruism from selfishness in a given interaction.

For instance, when one organism takes food from another, there is a positive fitness effect for one organism (the one gaining food) and a negative fitness effect for the other. Is this food sharing (altruism) or theft (selfishness)? It depends on who we think the actor is – looking back to Table 1 if the organism gaining food is the actor, we are in a (+, −) scenario and the behavior is selfish, whereas if we view the other organism as actively giving up the food, we are in a (−,+) scenario and the behavior is altruistic. We cannot generally make a determination which organism to consider the actor based on our observations; rather, we must import some assumptions about the causal structure of the interaction. This type of reasoning can be generalized to include many other kinds of social behaviors of interest, for example, host–parasite interactions or worker sterility affected by the queens in ant colonies.

This seems like a difficult problem to address, and the most productive way forward may be to view these categorizations as less than completely objective, and rather as having heuristic value (Halperin and Levy, 2022).[18] However, how much of an issue this is in practice is up for debate. Some situations may be clearer than others, where we can expect a general consensus who the actor is. For instance, we can often easily tell apart a case of food given freely to an other animal that is not demanding it (food sharing) from a case where an animal is

---

[17] For instance, we are often interested in classifying particular *actions* as altruistic, spiteful, and so on even though we often think of *traits* more along the lines of behavioral tendencies. What does that mean for studying the evolution of altruism – are we interested in traits or actions? Does this make a difference to our modeling evolution of social behaviors, or to how we individuate traits, and so on?

[18] One might be tempted to think of this as involving some underdetermination of causal factors by our evidence, but it is not clear to me that we ought to think of the issue in this way. The problem seems to arise, at least in many cases, based on how are inclined to define or conceptualize the trait under study – all the causal facts are the same, but in studying eusociality, for instance, are we studying a queen having sterile offspring (selfishness) or workers developing into sterile organisms (altruism)?

physically coerced into giving food (theft). Furthermore, for the purposes of observation and experimentation, heuristic value is likely good enough if what we care about is making things experimentally tractable.[19]

2.3.3 Additivity of Payoffs

So far, the issues we have discussed are issues for any concept of fitness we wish to employ in explaining the evolution of social behavior. There are, in addition, further complications that are specifically issues for inclusive fitness. Importantly, the calculations of inclusive fitness above assume additivity of payoffs, that is, that the total fitness effect from social interactions is simply the sum of the self- and other-effects of those interactions. In the context of game theory, this is often described as "equal gains from switching" (Nowak and Sigmund, 1990). When your strategy affects your fitness by some set amount, which combines additively with effects from your social partner, then the gains (or losses) from you switching from one strategy to another are the same regardless of what strategy your social partner has. For instance, in Table 2(b), switching from "Altruist" to "Not" always increases the focal organism's fitness by 1, regardless of which strategy their social partner has.

When talking in terms of quantitative genetics, payoff additivity is often related to Queller's "separation condition" (Queller, 1992b). Basically, when there are additive payoffs, we can separate selection gradients (which describe how phenotypes relate to fitnesses) from heritabilities (which describe how genotypes relate to phenotypes) in the way inclusive fitness requires. For more on this, see Queller (1992b), Marshall (2011), and Birch and Marshall (2014).[20]

While nonadditivity always complicates matters,[21] requiring additivity of fitness effects has been said to be a major drawback of the inclusive fitness framework, limiting its applicability and preventing its suitability for studying evolution of social behaviors (Nowak et al., 2010, Allen et al., 2013). However, others have debated just how much of a drawback the additivity assumption is. Among other things, it is possible to have an "expanded" inclusive fitness calculation (and a corresponding version of Hamilton's rule) that encompasses cases with nonadditivity (Queller, 2011).

---

[19] Thanks to two anonymous reviewers for raising these points.

[20] Birch (2016) points out that inclusive fitness calculations actually require satisfying two conditions, which he refers to as *actor's control* and *weak additivity* (p. 125–9), roughly that fitness effects on the recipient do not depend on the recipient's genotype/phenotype and fitness effects from all an organism's social interactions/partners can be added up. Only weak additivity is required to derive neighbor-modulated fitness, while neither condition is necessary for fitness calculations in general.

[21] For instance, models that take into account epistasis or dominant alleles are more complex than those that assume additive genetic effects. Thanks to an anonymous reviewer for this point.

Table 3 Nonadditive prisoners' dilemma

	Altruist	Not
Altruist	$b - c + d, b - c + d$	$-c, b$
Not	$b, -c$	$0, 0$

Consider a nonadditive prisoners' dilemma, shown in Table 3, where there is a synergistic benefit to mutual altruism. This synergistic component is often captured with an additional variable, d, that describes what happens differently when two altruists interact versus the case where there is only one altruist. (There are similar nonadditive games used to talk about spite. See, for example, Ventura (2019) and Heydon (2023).) One way to calculate the inclusive fitness of altruists in this game is to replace b and c in Eq. (2) with functions, B and C, that account for the synergistic effect (as in Okasha and Martens (2016b)):

$$-C = -c + d \cdot [r + p(1 - r)]/[1 - r], \tag{8}$$

$$B = b + d \cdot [r + p(1 - r)]/[1 - r], \tag{9}$$

where p is the frequency of altruists in the population. The exact form of these equations is not important for our purposes here. What is important is that the cost and benefit terms are functions of relatedness. It is awkward, at the very least, to talk about organisms being "causally responsible" for the synergistic term, and therefore for the costs and benefits as they are newly defined. Is this C really a self-effect and B an other-effect as we are supposed to have in inclusive fitness calculations? It seems not. So, some are unsatisfied with this way of extending inclusive fitness calculations (e.g., van Veelen, 2011).[22]

It is possible, instead, to keep the $rb - c$ aspect of inclusive fitness intact and write the inclusive fitness of altruists (again, as in Okasha and Martens (2016b)):

$$rb - c + d \cdot [r + p(1 - r)]. \tag{10}$$

Yet, you might think this does not really address the concern, as it still includes the d term, even if it is separate from the cost and benefit components. This

---

[22] You might also, in working within the quantitative genetics framework, define C and B as partial regressions, but there are concerns with that as well (Birch and Okasha, 2015).

isn't so much a concern about being able to write down the expression, but it can seem as if forcing things into an inclusive fitness formulation is overcomplicating matters without much explanatory benefit (Nowak et al., 2011)). (See Section 3.1 for more on the purported explanatory benefits of inclusive fitness.)

On the other hand, an inclusive fitness proponent might argue that this *does* address the concern because it isolates an evolutionarily important factor – the joint effect of the interaction of two altruists – that ought to be included in a causal model (Queller, 2020). This would be an important quantity to track in a situation where, for instance, both kin selection and greenbeard effects are occurring. Greenbeards confer some benefit on others with the greenbeard trait but not individuals who lack the greebeard trait, so the likelihood of receiving such a benefit depends on the frequency of greenbeards; d represents the benefit greenbeards confer on each other and $r + p(1 - r)$ represents the probability of interacting with another greenbeard. If greenbeard effects occur alongside kin selection, the fitness of altruists is then some combination of these greenbeard terms and $rb - c$, which is exactly what Eq. (10) captures. This argument applies more generally to combinations of kin selection with "kind" selection, where an organism's trait has different effects on their social partners depending on whether the social partners also have the trait, which includes greenbeard effects. See Queller (2011) for the full argument and explanation.

There are also ways to recover additivity, for instance by assuming weak selection – that gene frequencies are not changing or that the changes in gene frequencies are small enough to be ignored (Wild and Traulsen, 2007). This allows inclusive fitness calculations to be performed without extending or complicating them (see, for example, Grafen, 2006, Lehmann and Rousset, 2014). However, there are debates about whether or how much of a drawback assuming weak selection is. See, for instance, Nowak et al. (2011), Birch (2017a, 2019a) for some perspectives and discussion.[23] (We will return to the issue of weak selection in Section 3.1.4.)

2.4 Other Complications

So far, we have often been talking as if there is a gene for a social behavior, and an organism with that gene always exhibits the behavior toward another organism. There are at least four key assumptions here: that inheritance is straightforward, that organisms are haploid and asexual, that the behavior unconditionally expressed, and that there are pairwise interactions (i.e.,

---

[23] See also discussions of the explanatory value of Hamilton's rule as an "organizing framework," including cases where there is nonadditivity (Birch, 2017b, Koliofotis and Verreault-Julien, 2022).

interactions occur between two organisms at a time). None of these assumptions is true in general, and relaxing each of these assumptions makes inclusive fitness calculations more complicated. We will discuss two of these here, but other complications can be handled similarly, by complicating calculations to account for a more complex evolutionary scenario.

For instance, we might have a trait that is conditionally expressed, as is common, for example, in explanations of worker sterility or reproductive helping. In these cases, we treat the trait in question as conditional: "give help if such and such conditions hold," where those conditions will hold with probability p. For instance, one condition might be whether an individual is stronger than another. If that condition is met, will the weaker organism stay and altruistically help the stronger reproduce? The trait of interest would then be something like "taking the role of a helper rather than a reproductive when weaker than the existing queen." Another kind of conditional behavior would be found in cases of kin recognition, where organisms can (imperfectly, but often very accurately) recognize whether the organism they are interacting with is a genetic relative. Here, the trait would be something like "behave altruistically when interacting with an organism you recognize to be kin."

More generically, the trait of interest is whether the focal organism would help if the appropriate condition is met, and the consequence of having this altruistic trait is that there is some chance they will pay a cost c to confer a benefit b on their social partner. This makes inclusive fitness slightly more complicated to calculate, but it can be incorporated fairly easily, by noting that the altruistic behavior will only be exhibited, and therefore costs and benefits incurred/bestowed when the specified conditions are met, which happens with probability p (Frank, 1998). Therefore, we just weight $rb - c$ by the probability the altruistic action occurs:

$$\text{IF} = p[rb - c]. \tag{11}$$

Of course, if p is not constant as the population evolves, for example, if it depends on population structure and/or frequencies of traits in the population, this calculation will become more complicated as you will need to include an equation for p. However, that does not mean it cannot be done, and a similar concern would be raised for other methods of calculating fitness that would need to take into account the conditions under which the trait is expressed.[24]

---

[24] For instance, the neighbor-modulated fitness of altruists and non-altruists also include p:

$$\text{NMF}(A_i) = P(A_j|A_i)pb - pc, \tag{12}$$
$$\text{NMF}(N_i) = P(A_j|N_i)pb. \tag{13}$$

Other complications can be handled in inclusive fitness calculations as well. For instance, inclusive fitness calculations can be carried out with a diploid inheritance system, where organisms have two sets of chromosomes, or triploid, or octoploid, and so on. We can take this into account in inclusive fitness calculations, for example, by using a p-score for all the alleles at a locus or a breeding value that summarizes something like "genetic merit" for the trait of interest. To give an idea of how this goes: If using p-scores, we divide the copies of the allele of interest by the individuals ploidy (how many sets of chromosomes, and therefore alleles at each locus, it has) to derive a p-score, which captures the proportion of genes of interest at the locus (Grafen, 1985). So, if there is a gene associated with altruism, A, a homozygote with two copies of A would have p-score 1, a heterozygote with one copy would have p-score .5, and a homozygote with no copies would have p-score zero.[25] In inclusive fitness calculations, then, we look at genetic similarity in terms of correlations between p-scores of individuals rather than simply likelihood to share a single copy of the gene.

2.5 What Inclusive Fitness Is Not

One often sees inclusive fitness described as the sum of an organism's own payoff and its relatives' payoffs, weighted by a relatedness (or something similar, but phrased in terms of reproduction rather than payoffs). This "simple-weighted-sum" (SWS) method of calculating inclusive fitness is, of course, very different from the definition provided in Section 2.1. Recall that calculating inclusive fitness is often described as first stripping an organism's fitness of all the fitness effects from others, and then adding the fitness effects the organism confers on its relatives (Hamilton, 1964). By contrast, the SWS does not strip away anything and adds in all the social partner's offspring. For instance, in the prisoners' dilemma of Table 2(a), the SWS of an altruist who interacts with another altruist would be $(b-c)+r(b-c)$, including both organisms payoffs (the social partner's weighted by relatedness).

It is generally agreed that this is an incorrect definition (see, e.g. Grafen, 1982; Grafen, 1984b, Skyrms, 2002, Nowak et al., 2010, Birch, 2016, Okasha and Martens, 2016b, and Bruner and Rubin, 2020, for claims it is incorrect and explanations why). For instance, this heuristic has a well-known problem

---

[25] The p-score could be calculated in different ways, for example, by assigning a different number to each allele, then adding them up and dividing by ploidy. Also, different individuals in a population could have different ploidies, we could be interested in a p-score for a population rather than an individual, and so on (Grafen, 1985). The point is, this p-score construction can be used in a lot of different ways.

with double counting. Say we have two relatives, organism A and organism B, which interact and both have trait X. Under SWS, when we calculate the fitness of trait X, we count A's fitness twice: once when we consider A's contribution to the fitness of the trait and again (at least partially, depending on the value of r) when we take into account B's contribution to the fitness of the trait. We similarly double-count B's fitness.

However, SWS is often used as a heuristic method of calculating inclusive fitness. This heuristic use is extremely common, especially in the animal communications literature (see, e.g., Maynard Smith, 1991; Johnstone and Grafen, 1992, Johnstone, 1998, Nowak, 2006, Taylor and Nowak, 2007, Archetti, 2009a,b.) That is, it is often viewed as a useful heuristic for estimating the inclusive fitness of traits. One intuitive argument for why this heuristic should give an adequate idea of what evolutionary outcome to expect is this: If we are interested in tracking gene frequencies, adding the relatedness-weighted payoff of a relative to the focal organism's payoff means that the focal organism's genes will be passed on more often. In other words, SWS captures the fact that an organism in some sense cares about the payoff, or reproductive success, of its relatives. This is exactly the phenomenon that the relatedness parameter in inclusive fitness is supposed to capture. If using SWS gives us an adequate description of the evolutionary process, we should prefer it over more complicated calculations.

In addition, the heuristic at least allows one to calculate necessary conditions for something to be an equilibrium. In the late 1970s, the usefulness of the heuristic was debated in the context of the Hawk–Dove game, which captures competition over resources,[26] and it was determined that the heuristic sometimes gives the correct equilibrium predictions, and in other cases it lets you calculate necessary but not sufficient conditions for something to be an equilibrium.[27] That might not be so terrible, but the SWS heuristic is in many

---

[26] More specifically, in the Hawk–Dove game, there are two strategies, or types of behavior an organism can exhibit: aggressive and hawkish, or passive and dovish. Two doves will peacefully split a resource, while a hawk will take the resource from a dove. Two hawks, however, will get into a costly fight over the resource. The evolutionary prediction in this game is a stable mixture of hawkish and dovish behavior. Hawks do better when there are a lot of doves in the population. Doves also do better when there are a lot of other doves, though their fitness only exceeds that of hawks when there are a lot of hawks around; hawks benefit more than doves do from interacting with a dove, since they get the whole resource, but they suffer more from an interaction with a hawk than a dove does due to the costliness of the fight.

[27] The back and forth is roughly as follows: Maynard Smith (1978) argued that we could use the SWS heuristic method of calculating the inclusive fitness of organisms to predict the evolutionary outcome in the Hawk–Dove game played among relatives. Grafen (1979) showed that it depends on how the mixture of strategies in the population arises: When each organism is either hawkish or dovish, and there is some mixture of these two pure strategies in the population, the heuristic gives the wrong answer, but when all the organisms in the population are playing

ways worse when we want to know more than just the equilibria of the game. When we care about the dynamics of evolving populations, SWS can (quite dramatically!) mispredict the likelihood of different evolutionary outcomes (see Bruner and Rubin, 2020, who make this point in the context of animal communications).[28] So, we ought to remember that the definition of inclusive fitness given by Hamilton (1964), not the SWS calculation, is the proper way to think of and define inclusive fitness.

On the other hand, the SWS might be a suitable measure for studying long-term evolution when our explanations depend on "low-penetrance" (i.e., rarely expressed) genes (Fromhage and Jennions, 2019, Queller, 2019). In this case, whenever an organism exhibits the behavior associated with the gene, it is very likely that their social partner(s) will not, meaning the issues with double counting described above effectively disappear. This is similar to the weak selection resolution of nonadditivity issues described in Section 2.3.3; in certain cases, for certain purposes, complications and problems with definitions are not actually concerns. In many situations, these issues are not relevant for the work biologists do.[29] The important thing is to know when they *are* relevant, so we don't mess up our predictions and explanations in the many cases where things like nonadditivity and double counting need to be considered.

Additionally, though it is commonly described as such, I would argue that inclusive fitness is not usually well conceptualized as a property of an individual. For instance, Allen and Nowak (2016) argue that inclusive fitness is not a property of an individual because the c and b terms (i.e., the self- and other-effects) are generally partial regressions[30] (see also Akçay and Van Cleve,

---

mixed strategies (i.e., alternating between acting hawkish or dovish with some probability), the heuristic "amazingly" gives the right answer. The response by Hines and Maynard Smith (1979) was to grant that Grafen is right, but then show that for games with these sort of mixed strategy equilibria, the heuristic lets you calculate necessary, but not sufficient, conditions for something to be an equilibrium.

[28] One might object that double counting should not be an issue in animal communication because these interactions are asymmetrical, with one animal as a sender and the other(s) as a receiver. So, something like Queller (1996)'s discussion of not needing to strip fitness effects a reproductive gets from helpers when deciding whether to take on the role of a reproductive, contra Creel (1990), would lead us to conclude that stripping fitness effects from the social environment is not necessary. (Thanks to an anonymous review for raising this point.) However, in Queller's example, double counting is avoided because the helper "has never had the opportunity to express the genes under consideration, which are genes for accepting or rejecting the reproductive role, given that the bearer is the stronger partner" (p. 231). By contrast, in animal communications, animals usually take on both sender and receiver roles throughout their lifetime and we are not usually concerned to explain a choice of role.

[29] This might also help explain Grafen's finding that the SWS heuristic gives the correct result in models where each organism plays a mixed strategy, described in footnote 27. Thanks to an anonymous reviewer for pointing me to this discussion and relating it to the Grafen (1979) result.

[30] These measure correlation between two variables, holding other parameters/variables fixed.

2016) or correlations, not actual fitness effects, and synergistic effects of cooperation cannot be attributed to individuals. One might respond that, at least sometimes, regressions/correlations can be interpreted as causal effects on fitness (Spirtes et al., 2000, Lee and Chow, 2013, Birch, 2014a, Okasha and Martens, 2016a), and we have ways of determining an individual's contribution to a joint endeavor. Even so, c and b as used in evolutionary models employing inclusive fitness *are* generally conceived of as statistical, not causal terms. Moreover, relatedness is, at its heart, a measure of correlation between types within a population, not a measure of an individual's likelihood of interacting with different types of organisms. When relatedness is incorporated in this way, it makes it hard to see how inclusive fitness could be a property of an individual.[31]

Should we care whether inclusive fitness is a property of an individual? Is this an issue for the framework, as, for instance, Allen and Nowak (2016) seem to think? Well, it is not totally clear that our "standard" notion of fitness used in evolutionary models is a property of individuals in the first place. For instance, take the following argument by "statisticalists". There are different concepts of fitness we employ in biology. One of them, sometimes called "vernacular fitness", is certainly a property of an individual as it just describes the propensity of an individual to survive and reproduce. This might be of interest if we are studying, for example, individual lineages in a population.

Vernacular fitness, however, is not the concept of fitness generally employed in evolutionary models which aim to predict or explain how a trait takes over in a population, of which inclusive fitness models are one type. For example, models using inclusive fitness often aim to explain how altruism, cooperation, or spite might proliferate over an alternative trait. In this case, the statisticalists explain, we talk about fitness of traits, not individuals. These "trait fitnesses" cannot be easily translated into fitnesses of individuals, for example, because any individual has many traits that combine in order to affect their potential reproductive success, and so presumably should be treated as properties of classes or groups of individuals (i.e., trait types). That is, the concept of fitness we use in these evolutionary models, whether it is inclusive fitness or something else, is a property of populations or groups, not of individuals. (See, e.g., Matthen and Ariew, 2002, Walsh et al., 2017).

---

[31] Allen and Nowak (2016) further conclude that we should therefore not view individual organism as acting "as if" they are trying to maximize inclusive fitness. I am not sure this follows – viewing organisms as if they were maximizing something is a sort of analogical reasoning that does not depend on that something actually being a property of an individual. This reasoning and its relation to inclusive fitness will be discussed further in Section 3.1.2.

Of course, there is a whole huge debate on what fitness is, which we cannot do justice here. (That would be a separate book. See Otsuka (2019), for instance, on the role of mathematics in conceptualizing fitness and natural selection. Or, more specifically related to inclusive fitness, see Birch (2019a), on when inclusive fitness might be a property of an individual.) The point is that how much we care about whether inclusive fitness is a property of an individual depends on how we conceptualize fitness in the first place. A statisticalist might respond that *no* conception of trait fitness is a property of an individual, so, of course, inclusive fitness in these types of models is not a property of an individual. How much we care about whether inclusive fitness is a property of an individual depends also on what role we want inclusive fitness to play in evolutionary theory. We turn to that question now.

3 The Usefulness of Inclusive Fitness

Based on my presentation in the previous section, you might think the complications for inclusive fitness aren't so bad, but others take a more negative view. Given that there are complications for calculating inclusive fitness, some of which do not arise for all methods of calculating fitness (e.g., those surrounding additivity or pairwise interactions), it is worth asking: Can we simply do away with it? Is there a point to keeping around this inclusive fitness concept, despite complications?

This question was famously asked and answered in the negative a little over a decade ago (Nowak et al., 2010). That paper, however, generated enormous backlash with claims that its authors misunderstood inclusive fitness and why it was so important to understanding the evolution of social behavior. The replies included a response piece signed by over 130 scientists (Abbot et al., 2011).[32] Unfortunately, there isn't space in this short Element to get into this debate in detail. Fortunately, there are several other places to look for such a discussion and I have taken the liberty of putting some of them in a footnote for you.[33]

Instead of detailing each issue in the debate and the responses to criticisms, here, we will discuss one question that is in the background of much of the debate: What is gained by thinking of fitness as inclusive fitness? The most extreme positions on either side seem to be that inclusive fitness is an indispensable tool in evolutionary theory (e.g., West and Gardner, 2013) versus

---

[32] Another response was a (in my opinion very strange) YouTube video involving talking animated bears criticizing the authors of thinking of themselves as "important Harvard scientists" doing "important Harvard science."

[33] van Veelen, 2009, Nowak et al., 2010, Abbot et al., 2011, Marshall, 2011, Nowak et al., 2011, Strassmann et al., 2011, van Veelen, 2011, Birch and Okasha, 2015, Liao et al., 2015, Allen and Nowak, 2016, Birch, 2017a, Rubin, 2018, Woodford, 2019, Levin and Grafen, 2021.

inclusive fitness is mathematically suspect, adds nothing, and we should rid evolutionary theory of this framework (e.g., Nowak et al., 2010).

3.1 Benefits of Inclusive Fitness?

In the introduction, I said that inclusive fitness has generated important insights. As a historical note, at least, that seems to be true. Inclusive fitness theory has helped to give new, intuitive explanations of a variety of traits, including eusociality, the distastefulness of insects, parental care, genomic imprinting, and so on (again, see Grafen, 1984a, Marshall, 2015, and references therein). But that is separate from the question of what value it currently adds to evolutionary theory, and whether the benefits are just historically contingent on what people happened to find to be an intuitive explanation. What exactly is it that we gain from using the inclusive fitness framework? It is that question to which we presently turn.

3.1.1 The Phenotypic Gambit

One commonly discussed benefit of inclusive fitness is that it allows us to, in a way, incorporate genetics without knowing the details of how genetics influence the trait of interest. That is, it allows us to use the "phenotypic gambit": the idea (or bet) that we can make evolutionary predictions using information about observable phenotypes, effectively ignoring any information about underlying genetics (which genotypes are associated with which phenotypes, how many loci are relevant to the phenotype, etc.).

Of course, genetics do influence evolution. For instance, if the trait with the highest fitness is associated with heterozygotes (organisms with two different alleles at a locus), both alleles remain in the population and inheritance patterns prevent the population from converging on the phenotype with the highest fitness. However, often we just do not have the details of underlying genetics to work with, and many argue that in the long term, as new mutations emerge, these genetic constraints can be ignored (Eshel, 1996, Hammerstein, 1996, Marrow et al., 1996, Eshel and Feldman, 2001). Inclusive fitness allows us to incorporate genetic information that we often *do* have access to – information about genetic relatedness between social partners – while still making this phenotypic gambit with respect to genetic information we generally do not have access to – information regarding the underlying genetics of the trait (Queller, 1996).

Inclusive fitness can thus be a much more practical tool for those doing empirical work, and is seen as particularly helpful when interactions are asymmetrical and behavior is conditionally expressed (Levin and Grafen, 2019). For instance, if we look at a population and observe that poorly fed females are sterile and help well-fed relatives rear young, how do we explain this behavior?[34] When we think about the fitness of sterility genes that specify conditional behavior like "if poorly fed, take the helper role,"[35] it is hard to use neighbor-modulated fitness. The (well-fed) reproductive is not expected to express the altruistic helping behavior, regardless of whether she has those genes, because the conditions for its expression are not met. So, we can't just sum up the offspring of altruists versus non-altruists to determine when the genes will spread. Instead, we can look at inclusive fitness, track the consequences of the behavior when it is performed, and make inferences about the likelihood of the altruistic sterility genes spreading based on information we have about relatedness.

Though its usefulness in a phenotypic approach is viewed as one of inclusive fitness's major benefits, it also should be said that there is no reason that we *must* use a phenotypic approach with inclusive fitness. We are perfectly free to include additional genetic details. For instance, Rousset (2002) shows how including details regarding mutation rates can affect inclusive fitness calculations. Also, as will be discussed in Section 5.2, we can use inclusive fitness to study the details of genetic inheritance. (As a side note, evolutionary game theory is often considered a phenotypic approach as well (Hammerstein and Selten, 1994), but I see no reason why it must be – it is easy to incorporate genetics into evolutionary game theory and see cases where the phenotypic gambit fails (Rubin, 2015, 2016).) So, while inclusive fitness is useful in many cases because it allows us to incorporate genetics while relying on the phenotypic gambit, that is probably not the *only* reason people think it is useful.

3.1.2 Explaining the Appearance of Design

Many proponents of inclusive fitness argue we need inclusive fitness in evolutionary theory because it saves Darwin's insight that natural selection leads to the appearance of design (i.e., organisms appear designed to maximize their inclusive fitness). To give some historical context for this thought: Hamilton (1964, 1970) proposed inclusive fitness as a quantity that organisms are selected to maximize. It has since become a standard assumption that inclusive fitness is necessary in order to make sense of the appearance of design when it

---

[34] See Queller and Strassmann (1998, p. 167) for a description of this kind of example. Wheeler (1986) describes the inhibition and facilitation mechanisms, including environmental and nutritional factors, which influence whether organisms are sterile or in reproductive roles.

[35] It is best to think of this as a counterfactual conditional, not a material conditional. When the antecedent is not satisfied, we don't know the truth of the conditional (and hence whether the organism in question has the genes).

comes to explaining social behaviors. For instance, it is common to state that "inclusive fitness ... is a quantity that natural selection tends to cause individuals to act as if maximizing, just as Darwinian fitness tends to be maximized in the non-social case" (Grafen, 2009, p. 3137). Or, more explicitly stated, if we are going to think of organisms as maximizing agents, "doing so requires inclusive fitness" (West and Gardner, 2013, p. R579). This idea is so influential that biology students are commonly taught the principle that natural selection leads to organisms acting as if they are maximizing their inclusive fitness (Grafen, 2006, p. 559).[36]

We call traits which have the sort of functional role of promoting fitness "adaptations" and it is a goal of evolutionary theory to explain the appearance of these adaptations. It is, of course, possible to study evolutionary change without ever talking about adaptations by just calculating gene frequency changes, and so on. However, showing how natural selection can lead to the appearance of design is seen as the most important contribution Darwin made to evolutionary theory (Gardner, 2009). Some claim that, since inclusive fitness allows us to talk about social behaviors as adaptations, it is the only major development in our understanding of adaptations since Darwin proposed the theory of natural selection (West et al., 2011, p. 233), that it represents a "scientific revolution" (Rodrigues and Gardner, 2023), or that recent criticisms of inclusive fitness are irrelevant because inclusive fitness is the only concept of fitness that can play this role in explaining the appearance of design (West and Gardner, 2013, p. R582).

The basic argument for why only inclusive fitness can play this role is this: Organisms can only act to maximize things under their control, and inclusive fitness is the only fitness concept that only includes things under the organism's control. To elaborate a bit, organisms are in control of their inclusive fitness because they are in control of whether they confer the benefit on their social partner, but organisms are not in control of their neighbor-modulated fitness because they are not in control of whether their social partner confers a benefit on them. That is, neighbor-modulated fitness explains the evolution of altruism in terms of "statistical auspiciousness", or altruism happening to correlate with advantageous social neighborhoods. From a neighbor-modulated fitness point of view, if the organism could choose not to be altruistic, while keeping its social environment fixed, it would always stand to gain by doing so (Birch, 2016).

---

[36] The following, as well as many others, all express this basic idea: Grafen, 2006, Gardner, 2009, Grafen, 2009, West et al., 2011, Queller, 2011, West and Gardner, 2013, Okasha et al., 2014, Birch, 2016, Okasha and Martens, 2016b, Rodrigues and Gardner, 2023.

I have argued elsewhere, that, taken at face value, this "indispensability argument" for inclusive fitness cannot be right (Rubin, 2023). Granted, it seems intuitive to say that the production of the benefit is under the organism's control in the inclusive fitness calculation, but not in the neighbor-modulated fitness calculation, since in inclusive fitness we count the benefit the organism produces, whereas in neighbor-modulated fitness we count the benefit the organism receives. However, considering actions performed by other organisms is not generally thought to be a problem for the viewing organisms as having a "goal" of maximizing fitness; for example, we might consider the actions of predators in considering their prey trying to maximize their fitness or vice versa.

Additionally, inclusive fitness calculations do not just include costs and benefits, they include relatedness as a measure of correlation, which, recall from Section 2.5, is generally a statistical property of a population. In other words, the indirect fitness component of inclusive fitness is br, the benefit conferred times relatedness. In talking about control over benefits produced, we push relatedness to the side in considering the consequences of an organism's traits; in this context, relatedness is often glossed as capturing how much an organism values its social partner's reproductive success. This makes the indispensability argument appear much more straightforward than it actually is: The organism chooses whether to pay a cost c to confer a benefit b on a social partner depending on how much it cares about its social partners' reproductive success.

However, if we remember that relatedness is in fact a measure of correlation, we then have to decide whether the br term is under the organism's control.[37] This will only be the case when the organism is causally responsible for the level of correlation, r, for example, if its trait determines the traits of its social partners. However, if the organism is causally responsible for the level of correlation, it also has causal control over how likely it is to *receive* a benefit, that is, neighbor-modulated fitness is also under its control. So, inclusive fitness does not provide any additional benefit; we might just as well say organisms are acting as if they are attempting to maximize neighbor-modulated fitness. This is a similar point to that made by Rosas (2010): "if controlling assortment is the clue to controlling inclusive fitness and if the organism can be credited with it, the organism controls inclusive fitness and neighbor-modulated fitness in one move" (p. 8).

---

[37] Also, recall from Section 2.5, inclusive fitness cannot in general be thought of as a property of an individual. This does not automatically preclude us from talking "as if" organisms are maximizing fitness, but this whole argument is less clear when we talk about causal control of things that are properties of groups of individuals compared to properties of individuals.

One might object that this an *analogy*, a sort of metaphorical way to think of the organism as a maximizing agent using its phenotype to make sure its genes are represented in the next generation. The organism does not have to literally control inclusive fitness, but instead "chooses" b and c given r.[38] This is a natural response, and it puts us on the right track by compelling us to think hard about what the organism is choosing and what we are assuming is changed by that choice. Spelling out all the possible choice scenarios, or decision-making contexts, would take too much space for this Element (details are provided in (Rubin, 2023), Section 5), but we can go through an example to get a sense of things.

The decision scenario is usually described as choosing whether to perform some altruistic action or not, or how altruistic to be. If we think of the organism choosing b and c given some fixed r (and given some chance of the conditions being met for relevant behavior to be expressed),[39] as described above, we are imagining that the organism is likely to interact with organisms that share their genes, regardless of which choice they make. But r being fixed means correlation is fixed. So, we think of the choice from a neighbor-modulated fitness point of view, that the organism is choosing given some fixed level of correlation. And, if choosing altruism means you are more likely to interact with altruists, you should choose altruism, at least if the level of correlation is high enough relative to the b and c parts of the decision-making context. Put differently, if choosing some levels of b and c means you are likely to interact with others who have made the same choice, you can use a neighbor-modulated fitness calculation to determine what those levels should be.

While I don't think inclusive fitness can play this particular role, I do think it is useful for evolutionary theory. Let's consider some more options for an account of what inclusive fitness brings to the table that other fitness concepts do not.

3.1.3 Providing a Utility Function

Somewhat similar to the argument regarding maximizing inclusive fitness, Okasha and Martens (2016b) and Okasha (2018) propose that we can think of inclusive fitness as playing the role of a utility function in rational choice. That is, we ought to treat organisms as agents that assign utilities to outcomes

---

[38] Thanks to two anonymous reviewers for helping me to phrase and respond to this objection more clearly.

[39] To be clear, it cannot be that the organism is choosing b and c independently – they would choose to set b high and c at zero, and we would not get an explanation of altruism – but it could be that there is some exchange rate between b and c and the organism chooses how much cost to pay given the potential benefits they would confer.

based on the outcome for themselves and their social partners, as well as relatedness. Okasha (2018, p. 125) argues that, when r is a fixed parameter, we are licensed to switch from interpreting it as a measure of correlation to interpreting it as a measure of how much an organism cares about its social partner. We just assume that the population is adapted so that their way of valuing their social partners matches the level of assortment in the population. This licenses us to incorporate relatedness into payoffs, whereas in game theory we would normally not be allowed to include a measure of correlation in this way. (Correlations tell us about the probabilities of receiving payoffs, not the payoffs themselves.[40]) In this case, inclusive fitness gives us a utility function where the values assigned to outcomes do not change over time (at least in the additive case, with a constant r) and thus a constant goal organisms can strive for (Okasha, 2018, 130).

However, there are a few problems with conceiving of this as a benefit gained by thinking in terms of inclusive fitness. (Note: I am not claiming that Okasha and Martens are attempting to argue inclusive fitness alone allows us to talk in terms of utilities, see the next paragraph.) First, constant r is often a reasonable assumption, though not always. For example, Rousset (2002) demonstrates how r changes as the population composition changes when we account for mutation. (If you want a simple evolutionary game theory example of how r can change with changing population composition, you can look at (Rubin, 2018), Section 4.2.) Since relatedness is often defined as "whatever makes inclusive fitness work" (see, e.g., Marshall, 2011), we should not expect that stability is going to be a general property of r. Second, this reasoning does not extend to cases where there are nonadditive payoffs (Okasha, 2018), which, recall from Section 2.3.3, are important to consider.

Third, as Okasha and Martens (2016b) point out, inclusive fitness is not the unique fitness concept that has these desirable properties. There are other fitness concepts that can play the role of a utility function. In particular, they discuss how what they call the "Grafen 1979 pay-off" can provide an appropriate utility function. The utility assigned to each outcome in Grafen (1979)'s paper is a function of c, b, and r, but in a different way from inclusive fitness: An organism will interact with its own type with probability r and will interact with another type randomly drawn from the population with probability $1 - r$, and these interaction probabilities determine how likely they are to receive b. So, while inclusive fitness can sometimes play the role of a utility function in rational choice, it does not do so generally and it is not the only fitness concept to play this role.

---

[40] For further discussion of this in the context of inclusive fitness, see Rubin (2023), especially Section 4.

3.1.4 A Stable Criterion for Improvement

Birch (2017b, 2019a) argues that the distinctive value of inclusive fitness is in providing a stable criterion for phenotypic improvement throughout a process of cumulative adaptation.[41] That is, it provides us a consistent place to look to determine whether a new mutation, and associated change in trait, improves reproductive success of organisms.

When might we use a criterion for phenotypic improvement like this? Birch explains that there are two theoretical commitments that many people who argue for the usefulness of inclusive fitness adhere to: First, they view complex adaptations as their main explanatory target, and, second, they are committed to a Fisherian micromutationist view. That is, they have an empirical commitment to complex adaptations evolving through an accumulation of mutations, each of which has a very tiny effect on phenotype. He argues that thinking of these two commitments, we should not expect the distinctive value of inclusive fitness to lie in helping us calculate or understand short-term changes in gene frequencies.[42] Instead, in the context of explaining adaptation, there is a different sort of theoretical role for a fitness concept with respect to which inclusive fitness is superior: that of providing a stable criterion for phenotypic improvement over the evolutionary medium term. (Birch, 2017b, p. 134)

In thinking about the evolutionary "medium term," we are supposed to think of cumulative adaptation occurring over many episodes of short-term gene frequency change. A new mutant appears and spreads throughout the population, then another, and so on.

Here's the example of a process of cumulative evolution we are asked to consider, where multiple mutations occur successively, either affecting the reproductive success of the bearers of these mutated genes (i.e., the actors exhibiting the new behavior) or their social partners (who happen to be relatives):

1. In the first stage, a mutant is selected for marginal direct benefits to the actor.
2. In the second stage, a mutant is selected for marginal indirect benefits to a relative, despite direct cost to actor.
3. In the third stage, a mutant is selected for reduced direct cost to the actor.

---

[41] See also Lewens (2019) for a discussion of how "design" and "criterion for improvement" have historically been incorporated into evolutionary thinking.

[42] He initially talks about these commitments in relation to the assumption of weak selection, which is used to justify some assumptions used to calculate inclusive fitness (e.g., weak additivity, discussed in Section 2), and says that these assumptions make sense given these two commitments.

Birch argues that only the inclusive fitness of the actor provides a stable criterion for improvement over all these stages. The neighbor-modulated fitness of the actor cannot provide a consistent criterion because in stage 2 a mutation that detracts from neighbor-modulated fitness is favored. Likewise, we cannot look to the neighbor-modulated fitness of the recipient (i.e., the social partner of the mutant) because in stages 1 and 3 mutations that are either neutral or deleterious to the recipient could be favored. By contrast, in all these stages, the mutation positively affects the inclusive fitness of the actor.

This proposal is intuitively appealing, and it does not seem to fall prey to similar objections as the argument regarding the appearance of design, described in Section 3.1.2. However, note that it provides a more limited claim about the distinctive usefulness of inclusive fitness. First, we must be working within a micromutationist, gradualist framework of evolution. While micromutationist thinking is far from niche, there are many other types of evolutionary thinking and modeling. Second, we cannot say that neighbor-modulated fitness does not provide a criterion for improvement, just that inclusive fitness provides us a more stable place to look to determine whether a trait counts as an improvement.

3.1.5 Intuitiveness

It is possible that the distinctive benefit of inclusive fitness is simply that it is more intuitive than other conceptions of fitness (see, e.g., Maynard Smith, 1983). This might be true for some, but clearly others do not find the framework intuitive (e.g., Nowak et al., 2011). People seem to just find different frameworks more intuitive than others. Furthermore, just relying on intuitions can lead to confusions and incorrect conclusions.[43] At this point, we possibly ought to back up and take a closer look at how inclusive fitness relates to other concepts of fitness, particularly neighbor-modulated fitness.

3.2 Isn't It Just the Same Information Written Differently?

Different fitness measures often involve the same information, just organized in a different way. So, let's step back to ask a more general question: Why do we ever choose to write the same information in a different way? It is clear there is something to be gained from reorganization; scientists and mathematicians do it all the time to better convey information, but what is the epistemic value of doing this?

---

[43] Just look at the history of intuitions leading mathematicians astray (Hahn, 1980, Feferman, 2000).

Importantly for present purposes, inclusive fitness uses the same information about reproduction as standard notions of fitness, except that when, for example, an organism helps its relative reproduce, this is counted toward the helper's fitness rather than the fitness of the organism that produces the offspring. They agree completely on what the world is like (in terms of population structure, who reproduces and what their offspring are like, how trait frequencies change over time, and so on). From Figure 1 we know which smileys reproduce, who is causally responsible for each, and what traits these offspring have. We are just using those to calculate fitness differently for inclusive versus neighbor-modulated fitness. Along these lines, switching from a neighbor-modulated to inclusive fitness calculation can be thought of as a re-partitioning of causal effects (Frank, 2013).

In their shared domain, that is, when we've made suitable assumptions to guarantee our fitness calculations are correct, inclusive fitness and neighbor-modulated fitness give the same predictions for evolutionary change (Hamilton, 1970, Queller, 1992b, Taylor, Wild and Gardner, 2007, van Veelen, 2011, West and Gardner, 2013, Birch, 2017b, Rubin, 2018). If we are not identifying new causes or making new predictions, why do many biologists claim certain measures of fitness allow us to explain phenomena that others do not?

3.3 Should We Talk to Philosophers of Physics?

Maybe![44]

Philosophers of physics coming across the issues described in Section 3.2 might just see them as ruminations on equivalence, a topic many of them have thought a lot about. While many examples they discuss are, naturally, from physics, perhaps we can brave the wilderness of Hamiltonians (different Hamilton) and Lagrangians and try to find from them some guidance on how to sharpen our discussion. Here I will present just some initial thoughts on this, or a plausibility argument that there is something to learn from the philosophy of physics literature.

You can read the discussion in the previous section as an argument that, in many contexts, neighbor-modulated and inclusive fitness are equivalent – they agree completely on facts about the world and describe exactly the same states of affairs. They are provably equivalent within a domain of problems of interest.[45] Do these different ways of calculating fitness give us new explanations,

---

[44] Thanks to the following philosophers of physics for talking to me: Josh Hunt, Mike Schneider, Chris Mitsch, Elliott Chen, and Jingyi Wu. All mistakes are my own.

[45] There may be an argument to be made that the two are also *theoretically equivalent*. However, philosophers of physics disagree on how exactly to spell out what theoretical equivalence is

concepts, or understanding, despite being equivalent? There are different ways we might think to answer these questions.

We can think of inclusive fitness and neighbor-modulated fitness as reformulations of fitness. Within a shared domain, reformulations agree on the way the world is and so all the same information goes into the explanation. A classic motivating example of reformulations in philosophy of physics is the Hamiltonians and Lagrangians used to describe system dynamics in classical mechanics. One view on reformulation, which I think is useful for understanding what is going on with inclusive and neighbor-modulated fitness, is due to philosopher of physics Josh Hunt.

As Hunt explains, what we gain from reformulation is not new explanations – at least if we think of explanations as providing reasons why something occurs – but rather knowledge of *epistemic dependence relations* (Hunt, 2021a,b). These epistemic dependence relations tell us what we need to know to make particular predictions or solve particular problems. Different formulations then lead to different ways of solving problems,[46] and also different understandings of the same explanation (Hunt, 2021b, p. 6-7). Hunt calls this account "conceptualism", under which we can gain understanding through reformulation clarifying the epistemic structure of theories, in contrast to "explanationism", where understanding can only come from grasping explanations.

Since inclusive fitness and neighbor-modulated fitness include all the same information, they will give the same explanations for the evolution of social behaviors. For instance, in explanations of why altruism is favored by selection, reasons why altruism is favored will include high correlation, benefits outweighing costs, and so on. However, we generally need to know different things to calculate each of these. For inclusive fitness, we can use information about relatedness, for example, about how an organism's phenotype predicts their social partner's genotype. For neighbor-modulated fitness, we use information about how likely organisms are to interact with each behavioral type in the population, for example, about how an organism's genotype predicts their social partner's phenotype. We do not need to know about relatedness to calculate neighbor-modulated fitness, and we don't need to know about frequencies

---

(Weatherall, 2019). In any case, it's not clear that theories in biology (or physics, for that matter) are specified in such a way as to be amenable to an analysis of equivalence in terms of 1-1 mappings of semantic or syntactic content, or something of the sort.

[46] To use Hunt's example, we could reformulate the problem $|xy|$ to $|x||y|$. In the former absolute value calculation we first multiply x and y, then take the absolute value. To complete the first part, we use knowledge of the sign (+ or −) of these variables. In contrast, information about the sign is not needed to do the second calculation, since we take the absolute value as the first step, before multiplying (Hunt, 2021b, p. 10).

of interactions to calculate inclusive fitness (even if we could figure those things out with the information available to us).[47]

We understand explanations of social behavior arising out of these fitness calculations differently as well. Yes, high correlation can promote the evolution of altruism, but we can understand correlation either as a way of generating a sort of common interest (which we can see from inclusive fitness calculations, as r captures how much an organism gains from benefiting their social partner) or as leading to differential benefits for altruistic organisms (which we can see from neighbor-modulated fitness calculations). Both are true, but these different ways of understanding how correlation can affect evolution allow us a fuller picture of social evolution theory.[48] Therefore, pointing out that inclusive fitness and neighbor-modulated fitness merely have same information written in a different way does not undermine the claim that we have gained something by viewing evolution through alternative lenses; we just need to specify what has been gained, and conceptualism seems like it could be a promising place to look.

Philosophers of physics also talk a lot about the empirical significance of *symmetries*, features of a system that remain unchanged under some kind of transformation (see, e.g., Brading and Castellani, 2003), which will be relevant to our understanding of fitness calculations here. Philosophers of physics study when symmetries reveal empirical facts about the world; they often do, though the nature of the empirical facts revealed might depend on the nature of the symmetry. A simple example of a symmetry is rotating a sphere – you can rotate it around any axis and its shape stays the same. We (nonphilosophers of physics) often think of symmetries in terms of spatial objects being rotated or flipped and still looking like the same shape, but the symmetry concept is much more broadly applicable.

For instance, Galileo's argument for the rotation of the earth is an early example of reasoning using symmetries. As Brading and Castellani (2003) explain:

> His approach was to use an analogy with a ship: he urges us to consider the behaviour of objects, both animate and inanimate, inside the cabin of a ship, and claims that no experiments carried out inside the cabin, without reference to anything outside the ship, would enable us to tell whether the ship is at

[47] For a discussion of the interrelation between these calculations, using both the Price equation and replicator dynamics, see Rubin (2018).

[48] Something similar might be said about reformulation of evolutionary dynamics, using the Price equation, replicator dynamics, breeder's equations, and so on. Within a shared domain, these use the same information and reformulations agree on the way the world is (see, e.g., Page and Nowak, 2002), but point to different parameters that need to be estimated (e.g., selection differentials and heritability estimates versus payoffs and trait frequencies).

rest or moving smoothly across the surface of the Earth. The assumption of a symmetry between rest and a certain kind of motion leads to the prediction of this result, without the need to know the laws governing the experiments on the ship. [p. 5]

Because things would also look the same to us whether the Earth was rotating or at rest – their appearance is invariant under certain transformations of motion of the Earth, or "boosts" – we cannot conclude from observations of rocks falling in straight lines, and so on, an empirical fact that the Earth is at rest (Brading and Castellani, 2003, p. 4-5). Philosophers of physics have also discussed the empirical significance of "local" symmetries (transformations of subsystems) compared to "global symmetries" (transformations of the entire system) (Greaves and Wallace, 2014, Murgueitio Ramírez, 2020) or "duality symmetries" where two theories are shown to "generate the same physics" (Rickles, 2011).

Symmetries are important in biology as well, for example when it comes to evolutionary dynamics (Wagner, 2010, Huttegger et al., 2021).[49] For instance, we might learn that adding a constant to our measure of fitness does not change any evolutionary predictions (e.g., the speed of evolution or equilibrium predictions) when evolution is described by the continuous time replicator dynamics. These evolutionary predictions are symmetries: They are invariant (unchanged) as we transform fitness in a particular way (Huttegger et al., 2021). We can infer from this symmetry that, empirically, background fitness (as defined in Section 2.3.1) will not affect an evolutionary process that is well described by this dynamics.

We can also explore the symmetries revealed by the relation between inclusive fitness and neighbor-modulated fitness. When we transform our measurement of fitness by switching between inclusive and neighbor-modulated fitness, we can find that certain symmetries exist. Under certain assumptions, the direction of selection (i.e., which trait is favored by selection) will be the same under the Price equation (Hamilton, 1970, Queller, 1992b, Taylor and Gardner, 2007, Birch, 2017b) and both the direction of selection and speed of evolution will be the same under the replicator dynamics (van Veelen, 2011, Rubin, 2018, Huttegger et al., 2021). What might these symmetries teach us about the world of social behavior? Without more research, we can only begin to speculate.

---

[49] More readily apparent might be the importance of symmetry in morphology, where we can observe symmetry in body plans like a bilateral symmetry where the body is invariant under reflection (e.g., humans, flies) or radial symmetry where the body is invariant under certain rotations (e.g., starfish, many flowers). The morphology symmetries would be considered symmetry within a model, and the evolutionary dynamics symmetries would be symmetries between two different models of evolution.

4 What Is Kin Selection?

We now transition from the question of how to conceptualize fitness to the question of how to distinguish evolutionary selection processes. We are still going to talk about inclusive fitness, but now in comparison to a different, multilevel, fitness concept rather than comparing to neighbor-modulated fitness. The reason for this is that in this section we are going to discuss kin selection in comparison to group selection, and these two different fitness concepts (inclusive and multilevel) are important in the discussion surrounding these selection processes.

If you recall from Section 1, inclusive fitness is a method of calculating fitness, while kin selection is a type of natural selection. The two are often equated, though, because relatedness in inclusive fitness calculations is commonly thought of as a measure of the average kinship between interacting organisms. So inclusive fitness is often used when talking about kin selection for a trait, though it is widely acknowledged that r, and many methods for calculating r, can be thought of as general measures of correlation between types (Marshall, 2015). Sometimes people use the phrase "kin selection theory" to encompass inclusive fitness and kin selection, but many stress the importance of keeping these concepts separate as we will be doing here (see, e.g., West et al., 2011). For instance, it is common to talk about inclusive fitness versus neighbor-modulated as two different ways to conceptualize kin selection, as they are different methods of calculating fitness that we can use when describing evolution via kin selection (e.g., Rodrigues and Gardner, 2023).

That said, there are debates about how exactly to define kin selection, and in particular, how to distinguish it from what is called group selection. Roughly speaking, kin selection describes a selection process whereby traits are selected (at least in part) due to their fitness effects on genetic relatives. By contrast, group selection describes a process by which traits are selected (at least in part) due to the group membership of organisms bearing those traits. These rough definitions leave room for questions and debates regarding the distinction between kin selection and group selection: Are they merely different ways of conceptualizing the same evolutionary process (and if so, is one way better) or are they different evolutionary processes (and if so, how does one distinguish them)?

Some argue that kin selection is a special type of group selection (e.g., Sober and Wilson, 1999), while others argue we should think of group selection as a type of kin selection (e.g., Maynard Smith, 1976, West et al., 2007, 2008) and yet others provide ways to distinguish the two processes (e.g., Hamilton, 1975, Wade, 1978, Birch, 2017b, Okasha, 2020). We will look further into each of these approaches in turn. But first, we compare the inclusive fitness approach to the multilevel approach to calculating fitness.

4.1 Inclusive and Multilevel Fitness

When talking about mathematical frameworks for calculating fitness, we can compare inclusive fitness to the multilevel framework just like we compared inclusive to neighbor-modulated fitness. Though in this case, as we will see, these two methods of calculating fitness are thought to track, or more naturally capture, different selection processes. As mentioned, inclusive fitness includes both direct and indirect components (or self- and other-effects), and explains trait frequency changes by reference to both how many offspring are caused by an organism and how likely it is that these offspring are had by an organism with the trait of interest.

By contrast, in the multilevel framework the fitness of a trait is determined by both "within-group" and "between-group" components. If we wanted to write this out, similar to how we did for inclusive fitness in Eq. (1), we would have the following equation (which I am calling MLF for multilevel fitness, but is more usually called a multilevel partition or something similar):

$$MLF = \text{within-group fitness} + \text{between-group fitness.} \qquad (14)$$

The within-group component describes how interactions in the group affect the fitness of organisms with the trait. The between-group component describes fitness differences among groups, or how the group membership of an organism with the trait affects their fitness. The multilevel approach then looks at selection within groups versus selection between groups and explains changes in trait frequencies with reference to the difference between the two.[50] For instance, altruism can evolve when the between-group component is positive and large (groups with more altruists do better) compared to the within-group component, which will always be negative (altruists always do worse than non-altruists within a group).

Interestingly, these two approaches give equivalent predictions as to the direction of evolutionary change (Grafen, 1984a, Queller, 1992b, Frank, 1998, Lehmann et al., 2007, West et al., 2007, Marshall, 2011). Queller (1992b) provides a condition, now classic in the literature, for when inclusive and multilevel fitness approaches successfully predict evolutionary change: This is the separation condition mentioned in Section 2.3.3. That is, both approaches succeed under the condition of payoff additivity, and both fail (or, need to be

---

[50] For more on the multilevel approach, as well as group selection, see Okasha (2006).

extended) when payoffs are nonadditive. While Queller (1992b) provides this argument in the context of the Price equation, the same holds true in game-theoretic models (Birch and Marshall, 2014)[51] and more complicated models with finite populations and overlapping generations (Lehmann et al., 2007) – inclusive fitness and multilevel calculations are equivalent in that they successfully predict evolutionary change under the same conditions, and yield the same predictions for the direction and magnitude of evolutionary change.

These results, though, are about formal equivalence. These ways of partitioning fitness into two components – direct and indirect, or within group and between group – both track changes in frequencies of traits in the same way. However, this says nothing about the underlying selection process. We can use the multilevel approach to track changes due to kin selection, and the inclusive fitness approach to track changes due to group selection.[52] This leaves several questions remaining. We will address a few particularly important questions in this section. First, is kin selection just a type a group selection? Or, are there principled ways to distinguish the process of kin selection from the process of group selection? Is one more evolutionarily important than the other? Or, instead, is group selection just a type of kin selection? Finally, assuming we can distinguish the two processes, how does this relate to a preference for one method of calculating fitness over another?

4.2 Group versus Kin Selection

4.2.1 It's All Group Selection

Famously, Sober and Wilson (1999) and Wilson and Sober (1994) argue that altruism evolves through group selection, and that kin selection is a type of group selection.[53] Their reasoning is as follows. In evolutionary theory, we can distinguish between replicators and vehicles of selection (Dawkins, 1978). Replicators are the entities that are replicated and passed on generation to generation; in biological selection, these would generally be genes. Vehicles of selection, or interactors, on the other hand, are the entities whose features matter for determinations of fitness. So even though we might care about gene

---

[51] This model was originally presented by van Veelen et al. (2012) in an argument against Queller's equivalence claim.

[52] It should be noted, however, that there are detractors from this general view. See, for instance, van Veelen et al. (2014).

[53] They are responding to critics of what is sometimes called "old group selection" which was a way of talking about benefits to the group or group-level adaptations (versus group membership mattering to evolution of traits among individuals and individual-level adaptations), and was deemed in the 1960s onward to be not very evolutionarily important. For more on this distinction, see, for instance, Hull, 1980, Williams, 1985, Maynard Smith, 1987, Lloyd, 2001, Okasha, 2006, Grafen, 2008, Okasha and Paternotte, 2012, Lloyd, 2017.

Table 4 Prisoners' dilemma

	Altruist	Not
Altruist	1, 1	−1, 2
Not	2, −1	0, 0

frequencies, there is selection at the level of individual organisms because that's where the interactions that matter occur.

But, if individuals can be vehicles of selection, why not groups? If group membership is what is important for fitness, then we should also be able to consider group selection, regardless of whether groups replicate. Furthermore, it does not matter if these groups are "ephemeral" – for example, trait groups that exist for the length of an interaction (Wilson, 1975); organisms, too, dissolve after a period of time and we have no problem treating them as vehicles of selection.

Let's return to the prisoners' dilemma as an example of how we can think of interactions between organisms as involving groups (Table 4). In this case, pairs of individuals are treated as groups. Within groups, there is selection against altruism. That is, in altruist/non-altruist pairs, non-altruists have higher fitness (2 compared to −1). However, pairs of altruists have higher fitness than altruist/non-altruist pairs and pairs of non-altruists. Likewise, altruist/non-altruist pairs have higher fitness on average than pairs of non-altruists. The fitness of groups, that is, pairs of individuals, depends on the frequency of altruists in them.

So altruism evolves whenever the between-group selection for altruism outweighs the within-group selection against altruism. This can happen if altruist/non-altruist pairs are sufficiently uncommon – the within-group selection against altruists is weak because they are generally not in groups where there are fitness differences – which is to say whenever there is enough positive correlation. This is the same conclusion we would reach using the inclusive fitness or neighbor-modulated fitness approach, but importantly for Wilson and Sober (1994) the vehicle for selection is pairs of individuals. Those are what are causing fitness differences, not individuals.[54]

Under Sober and Wilson's way of conceptualizing group selection, kin selection is just a kind of group selection. When organisms tend to interact with kin, this just means that groups composed of all altruists or of all non-altruists

---

[54] For more on this, see Lloyd (2017) and references therein.

are more likely than they would be if groups were to be formed at random. This non-random assortment into trait groups is generated by relatedness since genetic relatives are more likely than chance to share traits. Or, as Wilson and Sober (1994) put it, "The coefficient of relationship is nothing more than an index of above-random genetic variation among groups" (p. 595). Kin selection merely appears different due to the different accounting procedure used for inclusive fitness calculations, not because there is a fundamentally different mechanism involved. Though this definition of group might be seen as "excessively liberal" (Maynard Smith (1998), discussed in Okasha (2001, 2002)), Sober and Wilson (1999) and Wilson and Sober (1994) have at least shown a way that every example of an explanation of the evolution of altruism can be conceptualized through the lens of group selection.

4.2.2 Two Different Selection Processes

Other authors disagree with Sober and Wilson, and argue that group and kin selection ought to be seen as distinct evolutionary processes. Even if one agrees with Sober and Wilson and believes that kin selection is a type of group selection, one might still want to acknowledge that there are distinct mechanisms, or different types of group selection, that we might want to talk about. If so, it would only be the categorization of the processes under the umbrella term "group selection" that is under dispute.

Maynard Smith (1964), who coined the term "kin selection," called the two "rather different processes." He described kin selection as the evolution of characteristics, which favour the survival of close relatives of the affected individual, by processes which do not require any discontinuities in population breeding structure (p. 1145) including benefits to offspring, siblings, or more distant relatives. While the population being divided into isolated groups, or partially isolated groups, may further enhance the evolution of prosocial behavior, such isolation is not necessary for kin selection to operate. This sort of definition of kin selection is used frequently, for example, by West Eberhard (1975):

> I shall use the term kin selection to refer to the subclass of natural selection by which genetic alleles change in frequency in a population owing to effects on the reproduction of relatives of the individual(s) in which a character (allele) is expressed, rather than to effects on the personal reproduction of that individual itself (the domain of classical selection). (p. 2)

Birch (2017b, 2019b, 2020) offers an account of the two processes broadly in line with Maynard Smith and West Eberhard's, claiming that those emphasizing equivalence of mathematical frameworks for calculating fitness (as described in Section 4.1) forget that kin and group selection were meant to describe two "*explicitly causal* hypotheses about the evolution of social behavior" (Birch, 2019b, p. R433), one about the role of genealogical kinship and the other about (partially) isolated groups. While in any particular empirical case these two factors may both be present, so that a distinction between which traits have evolved via group versus kin selection might not be completely sharp, it is important for our understanding of social evolution that we distinguish these two processes.

Birch's distinction between kin and group selection takes inspiration from Bill Hamilton and Peter Godfrey-Smith. First, on Birch's reading, Hamilton (1975) claimed that the distinction between kin and group selection was a matter of degree – some things might be clearly kin selection, while others are clearly group selection, but there are intermediate or mixed cases as well (Birch, 2017b, p. 93-4). Second, Godfrey-Smith (2006, 2008) distinguished between-group structured populations, where organisms interact within sharply bounded groups, and neighbor-structured populations, where organisms interact with their nearest neighbors in absence of any well-defined group structure (Birch, 2017b, p. 94). Again, this distinction is a matter of degree, and we might talk about of clustering or "groupiness" in a population (Fortunato, 2010).

Putting these two together, Birch (2017a) argues that kin selection occurs when relevant interactions occur among genealogical relatives and group selection occurs when there are well-defined social groups.[55] We can then fit selection processes into "K-G" space, according to how important kin versus group selection (high K versus high G) is in explaining the evolution of a particular behavior. Evolutionary processes that are high along the "K" axis are kin selection processes, while evolutionary processes that are high along the "G" axis are group selection processes. An evolutionary process that is high along both axes involves both kin and group selection, or "kin-group" selection, while one that is low among both axes involves neither. Rather, it involves some other mechanism, like a greenbeard effect.

To take some examples, social evolution in clonal colonies, which are isolated groups composed of highly related (because they are clones) organisms, proceeds via both kin and group selection (high K, high G). By contrast, we might think that populations with limited dispersal have some aspects of both kin and group selection, though to a lesser degree than clonal groups. When individuals tend not too stray too far from where they were born, this generates

---

[55] For full technical definitions of kin and group selection, see Birch (2017b), pages 97 and 99, respectively.

group-like spatial clusters. It also means individuals are more likely to interact with their relatives, who were also born or gave birth to them around that location (medium K, medium G). Populations in which everyone interacts at random involve neither kin nor group selection (low K, low G).

K and G often go together, as the above examples illustrate, but they can also come apart. When there are kin interactions but no spatial structure, there are no meaningful "groups" to divide organisms into (high K, low G). Additionally, models of human evolution often describe differences in between groups with limited migration, where the groups are generally assumed to be large enough that relatedness is low among individuals within them (low K, high G). (Though see Section 5.4 for an example of high K, low G human evolution.) In these cases, while we may be able to describe evolution using both the inclusive fitness and multilevel framework, Birch would say we can see different processes at work in each case. In the former, the process is aptly described as kin selection, and in the latter, group selection. There may be cases where we are unsure what to say, but that does not take away from the argument: "The distinction here is not sharp, but nor it is merely arbitrary or conventional" (Birch, 2017b, p. 101).

There are still other ways to distinguish kin and group selection. Wade (1978, 1985), for instance, gives an analysis along the same lines as Birch, appealing to different population structures underlying the two separate processes. Okasha (2020), on the other hand, uses causal graphs to delineate kin versus group selection. So, while there is a formal equivalence between inclusive and multilevel selection calculations, and either calculation can be used to describe evolution due to either kin or group selection, we do not therefore need to conclude that kin and group selection always describe the same evolutionary process (Birch and Okasha, 2015).

4.2.3 It's Mostly/All Kin Selection

Some argue that we should view social evolution through the lens of kin selection or that kin selection is a more important evolutionary force for explaining social behavior. These arguments sometimes have a different flavor from that provided by Sober and Wilson for the importance of group selection, as authors can agree that kin and group selection can be distinguished (possibly along the lines described in Section 4.2.2) but will defend an empirical claim regarding the relative importance of the two processes (Maynard Smith, 1998, Okasha, 2002, West et al., 2007).

For instance, Okasha (2002) argues that kin selection is of particular importance because whole genome relatedness prevents mutations that undercut the correlation mechanism. Let's say there is correlation between altruists due to a greenbeard effect. Then a mutation for a "falsebeard", which has the phenotypic marker of altruists but does not behave altruistically, could invade the population. Or, let's say there is correlation between altruists because they share a habitat preference, so they just happen to all live in the same place and interact frequently. (This would lead to a medium- or high-G situation as there will be clusters of individuals in different habitats.) Again, a mutation that leads to the same habitat preference as the altruists but without the altruistic behavior could invade the population.

As Okasha (2002) explains, in such cases there will be selection pressure at all other loci for genes that suppress the altruistic behavior while maintaining the habitat preference or phenotypic marker. Unless social partners are kin, altruists are no more likely than chance to share genes at loci other than the one containing the genes for altruistic behavior. So, a "modifier" gene – a gene that modifies the effects of other genes – that suppresses altruistic behavior would not affect the chance of copies of itself being passed on through the social partner reproducing. By contrast, if social partners are kin, relatedness captures the chances of sharing genes at all loci; this whole genome relatedness means that such a modifier gene suppressing altruistic behavior would be selected against for the same reasons altruism is favored. A modifier gene that suppresses altruism toward kin would prevent the organism from benefiting other copies of the modifier gene that are likely present in the social partner – it "will undermine its own replication prospects" (Okasha, 2002, p. 143). These modifier genes may not matter too much for short-term evolution, but in the long-term mutations can arise and we need to think about selection pressures at other loci. Non-kin selection mechanisms are less likely to lead to a stable sort of altruistic behavior.

This is an argument that kin selection is more likely to be evolutionarily important than other evolutionary mechanisms, including group selection, when it comes to the evolution of altruism. On the other hand, some authors take the opposite viewpoint of Sober and Wilson, and argue that group selection is a subset of kin selection. For instance, interestingly, though Maynard Smith (1964) emphasized that kin and group selection were two different processes, Maynard Smith (1976) argued that group selection was just a particular type of kin selection where specific group structures were present. This isn't necessarily a conflict, since the presence or absence of group structure can lead to different evolutionary processes, even if we think those processes are both types of kin selection, but it is at least a difference in emphasis.

West et al. (2007, 2008) argue that the group selection, while a potentially useful framework for analysis, often leads to confusion; the mathematics of taking a kin selection approach are often far simpler, leading to greater understanding and less time wasted. Now, this might strike one as merely a preference for a mathematical calculation of fitness (inclusive fitness over multilevel fitness), but these authors seem to claim more than that. In fact, they argue that there is no formal theory of group selection and that it is not "a general evolutionary approach in its own right" (West et al., 2008, p. 380) but rather a collection of particular models, limited in scope, and with limited connections between them. Furthermore, they see these problems not as a failure of the multilevel selection approach, but problems with the concept of group selection. Gardner (2015) develops a genetical theory of multilevel selection that overcomes some of these problems, but that he argues reveals a new problem: When populations are class-structured, for example, when different age groups or castes have different reproductive potential, it might not be possible to have a coherent notion of group fitness or group selection that encompasses the different classes within the group.

4.3 Same Information Written Differently (Redux)?

To return to what was said at the start of the section, we can distinguish between two different selection processes as well as two different methods of calculating fitness. We might have the same situation with inclusive and multi-level fitness as we did in the discussion at the end of section 3 with inclusive and neighbor-modulated fitness – it's just the same information about who reproduces how much, but written in different ways. However, we might also think that something just *seems* different about this case. Inclusive and neighbor-modulated fitness are used to describe the same evolutionary processes, and the arguments surrounding their usefulness do not tend to be wrapped up in arguments about whether group or kin selection is at play. Does this raise different epistemological questions regarding their role in social evolution theory?

There are a couple things to emphasize in attempting to come up with an answer. The first thing to emphasize is that there are different underlying processes we might care about; even if one thinks they are all varieties of group selection or all varieties of kin selection, it is easy to recognize that there are different things going on in group structured populations versus well-mixed populations where altruists can recognize kin and direct their altruistic actions toward them. Mechanisms having to do with interactions among kin might be important to focus in on sometimes because they lead to sort of stability of altruistic traits that is distinctive, as described in Section 4.2.3 (Okasha, 2002, West et al., 2007, 2008, Birch, 2020). By contrast, we might want to focus on interactions in group-structured populations if we are studying the emergence of higher-level entities, for example, the transition from a group of single-celled organisms to a multicellular organism (Michod, 2000, Godfrey-Smith, 2009, Queller and Strassmann, 2009, Clarke, 2013, Birch, 2020).

The second thing to emphasize in this discussion is that there are fitness calculations that seem more natural depending on which process we think is occurring. Inclusive fitness is generally thought to be a more natural way to calculate fitness when interactions among kin are important to selection because it organizes around a parameter, relatedness, that can easily summarize facts about kin, that is, how related they are. Likewise, the multilevel fitness partition is generally thought to be a more natural way to calculate fitness when group structure is important to selection since it organizes around facts about group structure we are already investigating.

With these things in mind, let's return to conceptualism, as discussed in Section 3.3. Recall that reformulations agree on the way the world is (within their shared domain) and that, according to conceptualism, what we gain from reformulation are not new explanations but knowledge of epistemic dependence relations (Hunt, 2021a,b). These epistemic dependence relations then tell us what we need to know to make predictions or solve problems, where different formulations lead to different ways of making predictions or solving problems.

In the case of inclusive fitness, we need information about self-effects, other-effects, and relatedness. For multilevel fitness, by contrast, we need information about within-group and between-group fitnesses and variances. Like with inclusive versus neighbor-modulated fitness, these two frameworks require us to know different things to calculate fitness, so may be more or less easy to use to make predictions about evolutionary change based on what is easy to measure or calculate in a population of interest (even if we could figure out the relevant information to make either calculation based on what we know).

So far, this is similar to what we said about inclusive versus neighbor-modulated fitness. The difference here is that the different fitness calculations are more naturally suited to capturing different selection processes. Is this merely an instrumental or pragmatic consideration, having to do with ease of use, or is there more we can say? Hunt (2022) describes these naturalness considerations as epistemic or "intellectual" rather than instrumental. To see why, we need to elaborate a few more details of his view.

First, he argues that epistemic dependence relations form the basis of a problem-solving plan, for example, we plan to predict evolutionary outcomes by looking at the difference in strength of between-group versus within-group selection. Second, he argues that expressions or formulations can "wear on their sleeves" certain properties that others do not. There is a technical definition of

these "sleeve properties" (p. 159), but roughly we can think of this as meaning that anyone who understands the model should infer that the property is
present. In case where one formulation wears some relevant properties on its
sleeves, there is epistemic or intellectual value in that formulation because it
rules out potential solutions to the problem that some other formulation does
not (p. 173–4).

Philosophers of physics talk about manifest properties (a subset of sleeve
properties) in discussions about physics things like Yang-Mills theory and
quantum two-body problems, but let's stick with our biology. If we want to
figure out whether between-group selection for altruism is stronger than within-
group selection against altruism – that's the problem to be solved – a multilevel
fitness calculation makes manifest how fitness depends on this group structure,
where an inclusive fitness calculation does not. That is, the multilevel fitness
calculation wears on its sleeve the relative strength of selection pressures within
versus between groups, a property of a model or population of interest. Anyone who understands the multilevel fitness calculation ought to immediately
make inferences about this property. By contrast, the inclusive fitness calculation of altruism will not wear this property on its sleeves. We might be able
to conclude that between-group selection for altruism must be stronger than
within-group selection against altruism when the inclusive fitness of altruists
is positive, but this requires additional knowledge of equivalence results or
further calculations; we would have to perform an additional translation of one
fitness expression into another (in effect moving to the multilevel framework),
or construct intermediary expressions to make determinations about the relative
strengths of selection.

This might sound somewhat simple or artificial, but we can at least imag-
ine there are phenomena in the world where exactly what we are tracking is
all about inter- versus intra-group dynamics. In addition, it might shed some
light on debates over whether it is "really" all group selection or all kin selection, that is, debates about which selection process is fundamental. We might
think of these positions as metaphysical views about fundamentality – which
process is more fundamental? Broadly speaking, if these metaphysical views
are associated with mathematical reformulations, the positions might be (met-
aphysically) equivalent or else we might need to bring in further metaphysical
resources to privilege one view over another and call it fundamental (Rosenstock et al., 2015, Wu and Weatherall, 2024).[56] However, in Hunt (2022)'s

---

[56] Rosenstock et al. (2015) tie ongoing debates about theoretical equivalence with debates about
structure. I leave aside discussions about structure, but note that group selection models are
sometimes said to have "more structure" than kin selection models. Group selection models

point of view, "physicists' talk about fundamentality in terms of their attitudes toward privileging some formulations or variable choices over others" (p. 181). We may not need to wade into metaphysics to talk about fundamentality after all.

Ultimately, we will not resolve these debates here. Instead, we will move on to a different approach to thinking about the usefulness of kin selection and discuss examples where kin selection explanations have been illuminating of various social phenomena.

5 The Importance of Kin Selection

We began this Element with familiar, intuitive examples of social behaviors to motivate our discussion of social evolution. But social evolution is much broader than the range of those examples might imply. Now, we will put the versatility of kin selection explanations on display. We will start with the so-called haplodiploidy hypothesis, which is a classic example and historically important in the social evolution literature, and related research on split sex ratios. Then, rather than merely rehashing all our motivating examples in further detail, we will turn to some examples that are maybe less well known – genomic imprinting and filial cannibalism – in order to give a broader sense of the uses kin selection has been put to in explaining a range of phenomena. Finally, we will examine another familiar example, human altruism, and discuss the group versus kin selection debate in that context.

This, of course, does not exhaust what we could say about the importance of kin selection, nor does it represent all the best evidence available to us. There is plenty of evidence that kin selection is evolutionarily important. For instance, kin discrimination, where help is preferentially given to closer relatives, has been found in many species (Fletcher et al., 1987, Mateo, 2002, Griffin and West, 2003, Starks, 2004, Strassmann et al., 2011) and the level of kin discrimination depends on the benefits of helping behavior (Griffin and West, 2003). There is evidence that relatedness in groups of cells is predictive of both the level of sociality in the group and the likelihood that the group will make the transition to a multicellular organism (Fisher et al., 2013). There is a positive correlation between relatedness and the number of genes associated with cooperation, across a range of species of microbes (Simonet and McNally, 2021), and manipulating relatedness levels experimentally in microbes shows

---

partition into between- versus within-group selection processes, where kin selection models look at the fitness of individuals and do not partition into two separate processes in the population (Shavit and Millstein, 2008). Maybe there are more insights to be gleaned from philosophy of physics in this regard.

that higher relatedness leads to higher levels of cooperation after a period of evolution (Griffin et al., 2004).

The examples below were chosen based on illustrative value rather than strength of evidence. There are important historical debates (and confusions) surrounding the connection between haplodiploidy and kin selection. The genomic imprinting example, I think, provides a clear example of why sleeve properties (Section 4.3) are relevant to the discussion of the importance of kin selection. Filial cannibalism illustrates another case where our intuitions might impact our classifications of social behavior (as in Section 2.3.2). And, the discussion of broad-scope human altruism gives us a worked out example to test intuitions regarding the kin versus group selection debates (Sections 4.2.1–4.2.3).

5.1 Haplodiploidy

The history of debates over the usefulness of inclusive fitness and kin selection is intertwined with debates over the haplodiploidy hypothesis. The original thought was that a particular kind of altruistic behavior, eusociality, was driven by a haplodiploid sex determination system because of the higher relatedness it can generate (Hamilton, 1964, 1972).

To have in mind as a baseline for comparison, in diplodiploid species, where all organisms have two sets of chromosomes, an offspring gets one set of genes from each parent. The relatedness of offspring to parents, and among full siblings, is $1/2$. Thinking of relatedness as identity of genes due to common descent gives intuitive explanations why. Offspring receive half of their parents genes, so they will share $1/2$ of their genes. The probability of full siblings sharing a gene that is identical by common descent is also $1/2$; the likelihood they received the same allele from each of their mother or father is $1/2$ across loci. For instance, if the mother's genotype is Aa, there is a 50% chance of sibling 1 receiving the A allele, and a 50% of it receiving the a allele. These chances are the same for sibling 2. So, the chance they both receive the A allele is $1/2 \cdot 1/2 = 1/4$. Likewise, the chance they both receive the a allele is $1/2 \cdot 1/2 = 1/4$, for a total chance of receiving the same allele (whether its A or a) of $1/2$. The calculation is the same for the chance of receiving the same allele from the father.

In haplodiploid species, by contrast, some organisms (the males) are haploid, with one set of chromosomes, and some (the females) are diploid, with two sets of chromosomes. This type of sex determination is found in some insects, including ants, bees, and wasps. This generates new patterns of relatedness. In a nest or hive with one queen (female who mates) who only mates once, relatedness among sisters is 3/4, compared to the 1/2 generated among full siblings in diplodiploid organisms. This is because they all inherit the same alleles from the father – he only has one set to pass on. So, across loci, they will share 100% of the genes from their father, and 50% of the genes from their mother, for an overall relatedness of 3/4. This higher level of relatedness is sometimes called "supersister" relatedness (Kennedy and Radford, 2020). (Brothers in haplodiploid species are related to each other by 1/2 since they develop from unfertilized eggs and only inherit genes from their mother.)

Because haplodiploidy increases relatedness between sisters in a nest or hive, it has historically been seen as promoting the evolution of eusociality, which (you may recall from Section 1) is a social system in which there is a division of reproductive labor where some organisms do not reproduce. Commonly, in eusocial colonies, there is one queen who reproduces, and a number of female workers who do not. Female workers give up reproductive opportunities (or are prevented from reproducing via development or control mechanisms), incurring a cost to benefit the colony as a whole by helping to defend the colony and raise offspring. So, eusociality evolves via kin selection: Giving up reproductive opportunities can evolve because the benefits of it fall differently on highly related individuals. From an inclusive fitness point of view, the worker helping her mother to produce more of her sisters (to whom she is related by 3/4) is more beneficial than her producing her own offspring (to whom she would be related by 1/2, as she would pass on half her genes).[57]

Hamilton therefore suggested what became known as the haplodiploidy hypothesis, the hypothesis that haplodiploidy promotes eusociality, or aid-giving behavior by females in a colony more generally (Hamilton, 1964, 1972). Over the years, there have been multiple problems raised for the haplodiploidy hypothesis. We'll go through just a few. First, though workers are related to their sisters by 3/4, they are only related to their brothers by 1/4 (West Eberhard, 1975). (This relatedness calculation takes into account the fact that males pass on fewer genes: We multiply the relatedness of 1/2 by their reproductive value of 1/2 that of females to get 1/4 (Grafen, 1986).) This means the average relatedness of a worker to those she is helping in the colony is only 1/2, the same as relatedness between full siblings in diplodiploid species. Maybe the workers invest more in helping their sisters (Trivers and Hare, 1976). Could be, but then there would be conflict of interest between them and their mother,

---

[57] A colony with multiple reproducing females or whose queens have multiple matings for the single female would have lower relatedness among workers. It depends on the specifics on whether relatedness among sisters would still be higher than the 1/2, e.g., if non-queens only occasionally get to reproduce, average relatedness among workers would still be high.

who would want help for all her offspring (Trivers and Hare, 1976, Gadagkar, 2019). So, the difference between supersister relatedness in haplodiplods versus sister relatedness in diploids (by itself) is likely inadequate to explain the evolution of eusociality (West Eberhard, 1975, Hunt, 1999, Gadagkar, 2019). (However, this objection has recently seen some pushback from a number of angles, for example, by suggesting that sisters receive greater benefits than brothers from the same amount of help, increasing the benefits toward sisters without biased helping behavior (Rautiala et al., 2019, Kennedy and Radford, 2020).)

Second, eusociality occurs in many species outside haplodiploid organisms. The first evidence of eusociality was mainly found in haplodiploid organisms, making the haplodiploidy hypothesis seem well supported. Since the 1960s and 1970s, however, eusociality has been found in many other insects, in some species of shrimp, in mammals like naked mole rats, and arguably even in some species of plants (Thorne, 1997, Burda et al., 2000, Duffy et al., 2000, Burns et al., 2021). Third, relatedly, there are many haplodiploid species that have not evolved eusociality, further breaking the connection between haplodiploidy and eusociality (Wilson, 2008, Nowak et al., 2010). In fact, there seems to be no significant correlation between the sex determination system (haplodiploid versus diplodiploid) and eusociality (Nowak et al., 2010).

People may debate what this means for inclusive fitness or kin selection (see, e.g., Gadagkar (2019), or Nowak et al. (2010) compared to Ross et al. (2013)), particularly because it has been acknowledged from the start that other factors (affecting costs and benefits) are important in addition to relatedness. It might be that there is only a historically contingent link tying the haplodiploidy hypotheses to the motivation for these two concepts and justification of their usefulness (West Eberhard, 1975). Kin selection has also been used in alternative explanations of the evolution of eusociality, such as ecological explanations (Ross et al., 2013), or explanations focusing on life insurance or fortress defense (Queller and Strassmann, 1998).

Haplodiploid inheritance systems and the relatedness patterns they generate are still an important part of the evidence for the evolutionary importance of kin selection, however. Better support for kin selection can be found by studying split sex ratios in haplodiploid social insects, where there are groups that produce systematically different sex ratios. (See Grafen (1986) for a theoretical analysis and a history of these ideas.) In diploids, the sex ratio is predicted to be 1:1 at equilibrium (Fisher, 1930). Both sexes prefer the same ratio as the relatedness among parents and offspring, or all siblings, is all $1/2$. By contrast, in colonies with one queen who mates only once, relatedness of workers to sisters is three times that of their relatedness to brothers ($3/4$ versus $1/4$), meaning they prefer the sex ratio to be 3:1 in favor of females, in comparison to queens who prefer the sex ratio to be 1:1 (Trivers and Hare, 1976). (There are, of course, assumptions involved in arriving at these numbers.[58])

As this "relatedness asymmetry" decreases – for example, because the queen mates more than once or there are multiple queens, both of which decrease the relatedness of a worker to her sisters – the workers' preferred sex ratio decreases as well. In species where workers (at least partially) control the sex ratio, there is a predicted correlation between relatedness asymmetry and female bias in sex ratios. In a meta-analysis of the social *Hymenoptera*, Meunier et al. (2008) find that, indeed, the sex ratio is split, where there are systematically different sex ratios produced depending on the degree of relatedness asymmetry in different colonies or populations, consistent with previous studies (Queller and Strassmann, 1998, Chapuisat and Keller, 1999, Mehdiabadi et al., 2003, Bourke et al., 2005).[59]

Though the history of debates over kin selection's place in evolutionary theory is tied to the haplodiploidy hypothesis, the importance of kin selection does not rest solely on the shoulders of haplodiploid species. There are other uses of kin selection in explanations of social behavior. Many of these were described in the start of Section 5. We turn now to some others.

5.2 Genomic Imprinting

Genomic imprinting is a process whereby genes are turned off or on depending on whether they've been inherited from the mother or father. This process is epigenetic, that is, it is an inheritance process that does not involve changes to DNA structure. In genomic imprinting, gene expression is controlled by factors that can be erased and reset, for example, by attaching methyl groups to important areas of the DNA strand, changing its structure such that transcription factors can no longer bind to it properly. It is important that these methyl groups can be removed and added throughout a lifetime, so that the imprint can be erased as reset depending on the allele's environment, including whether it is being passed on by a male or female organism. Though it might be awkward to call genomic imprinting a "behavior", there are fascinating kin selection explanations of patterns of gene expression based on maternal versus paternal inheritance, in large part built on the work of David Haig.

---

[58] For instance, all of this assumes there is no difference in the cost of producing males and females. If costs are different, we would better say workers prefer a 3:1 ratio of investment in females versus males. Other factors make things more complicated, but the underlying logic stays the same.

[59] There are arguments arising out of this sex ratio research that haplodiploidy could influence the evolution of sib rearing (e.g., Trivers and Hare (1976)), which have been shown to depend on the sex ratios being split, Grafen (1986).

Following Queller (2003) and Patten et al. (2014), let's call alleles inherited from a mother "matrigenic" and alleles inherited from a father "patrigenic" (to distinguish them from the mother's and father's genes, which may have different methylation patterns). These matrigenic and patrigenic alleles can have different patterns of relatedness. That is, there is sometimes asymmetric relatedness (Haig, 2000b, 2002). For instance, if females reproduce with more than one male throughout their lifetime, a matrigene has higher relatedness than a patrigene to any future offspring of their mother. Those future offspring could possibly be full siblings (having the same mother and father, with relatedness 1/2) or maternal half siblings (having the same mother, but a different father, for relatedness 1/4).

So, in this kind of situation, we would expect that the patrigene expresses less altruistic behavior toward the mother, namely, behavior that forgoes making use of maternal resources in development in order to allow them to be invested in future offspring. So, fetal growth enhancers are expressed more often in patrigenic alleles and fetal growth inhibitors more often in matrigenic alleles (Mochizuki et al., 1996). And, patrigenic alleles promote the development of behaviors like frequent waking at night to feed (Haig and Wharton, 2003, Haig, 2014). The rate of multiple paternity can be thought of as a "discounting" factor for the patrigenic allele's inclusive fitness benefits from altruistically not using up maternal resources (Haig, 2000b, p. 15). Since relatedness is lower, the inclusive fitness benefits to the patrigenic allele of fetal growth inhibitors are lower, and so we see fetal growth enhancers expressed. In fact, we may see a sort of "parental antagonism" where the expression of a fetal growth enhancer increases the inclusive fitness of a patrigenic allele while decreasing the inclusive fitness of the matrigenic allele (Haig, 1997).

Multiple mating is only one source of asymmetric relatedness; dispersal patterns can affect relatedness asymmetrically as well (Haig, 2000a, Van Cleve et al., 2010, Brandvain et al., 2011, Úbeda and Gardner, 2011).[60] For instance, if male offspring tend to disperse, then organisms tend to interact with matrilineal (i.e., its mother's) kin. If male offspring tend to disperse, *and* mating tends to be with a single male in the area (until is he is ousted and replaced by a different male), then organisms will tend to interact with their patrilineal kin in their own age group – that is, there will be a lot of paternal half siblings about – but matrilineal kin from older age groups (Haig, 2000a). Imprinting can affect behaviors relevant to different types of interactions differently, depending on what class of organisms those interactions tend to be with.

---

[60] Kin selection has also been used to explain the evolution of this dispersal in the first place, e.g., because it reduces competition over resources among kin (Hamilton and May, 1977).

This, to me, seems like a case where sleeve properties (discussed in Section 4.3) are clearly relevant to understanding the type of evolutionary explanation we are inclined to give, using inclusive fitness and based on kin selection. There is a puzzle to solve – why is there differential imprinting depending on which parent an allele was inherited from? – where we want to pick a fitness calculation that wears on its sleeves facts about inheritance patterns. There are certain solutions to the problem immediately ruled out by thinking about the inclusive fitness of expressing fetal growth enhancers and inhibitors. For example, we are never going to consider the patrigene gaining more from fetal growth inhibitors than the matrigene would; this wouldn't make sense unless the father was somehow more related to the mother's future offspring than the mother is, which is not possible given the inheritance system described. Furthermore, anyone who understands the facts described here about relatedness asymmetry and the costs and benefits of using up certain maternal resources should be able to clearly see when certain properties (e.g., fitness advantages of imprinting patterns) are present. By contrast, other fitness concepts would make the connection between inheritance patterns and the existence of those properties more opaque.

5.3 Filial Cannibalism

Filial cannibalism refers to the phenomenon where parents eat their own offspring. This puzzling behavior seems to lower fitness – if you eat your offspring you therefore have fewer offspring. However, filial cannibalism exists in diverse species, including fishes, reptiles, insects, birds, and mammals (Bose, 2022). Furthermore, it commonly coexists with parental care (Polis, 1981, Klug and Bonsall, 2007). What conditions would lead to parents eating their offspring, when clearly it is in their interest for those offspring to survive?

There can be direct fitness benefits of filial cannibalism, for example, gaining nutrients to benefit future reproduction. A parent needs energy to maintain themselves while protecting their offspring, so eating a few of their current offspring may allow them to maintain their health sufficiently to survive to reproduce again, netting more offspring overall (FitzGerald, 1992, Manica, 2002). (Recall from Section 2.3.2 that lifetime fitness is important for evolutionary change.) While this explanation has some support, there is also evidence against it. For instance, in threespine sticklebacks, there does not seem to be a relationship between number of eggs eaten and amount of food they have already consumed; experimenters found that providing some of these fish with extra food rations compared to others did not decrease their egg consumption (Belles-Isles and FitzGerald, 1991). This energy/consumption explanation is likely not the whole story.

There are also explanations that may be given in terms of kin selection. For instance, filial cannibalism can remove less healthy offspring to free up more space or resources for healthy offspring, making them more likely to survive to reproductive age (Klug et al., 2006). From the perspective of a kin selectionist, this might be thought of as analogous to parental care, as parents sacrifice their own current reproductive numbers to increase the fitness of their offspring, to whom they are highly related. Though it does not seem particularly common to explain filial cannibalism with reference to kin selection,[61] Garay et al. (2016) make the point (in the context of sibling cannibalism) that we can view this sort of behavior through the lens of kin selection, where there is a sacrifice by one organism to increase the reproductive success of kin.

Furthermore, Klug and Bonsall (2007) develop a mathematical model that shows how the level of filial cannibalism depends on both among-offspring relatedness and resource competition in a brood, as well as several other factors. The level of relatedness depends on how mating occurs, for example, whether the brood is from a single mating or multiple – relatedness is higher when all the offspring in a brood are full siblings, and lower in mixed broods (with more half siblings). To take one result from the paper to demonstrate the usefulness of kin selection in this context, they find that filial cannibalism is likely to evolve when among-offspring relatedness is high and offspring competition increases as relatedness increases.[62] The benefits of this behavior, reduced competition over resources, fall on highly related individuals. If resources are limited, the benefits of reduced competition may be sufficient to outweigh the cost of giving up immediate numbers of offspring, and filial cannibalism may evolve via kin selection.

Though I find these arguments plausible, it is, to me, frankly, weird to think about cannibalism as altruistic. I suspect this has something to do with my intuitions regarding the recipient of the action. In Section 2.3.2, we discussed examples from Halperin and Levy (2022), which demonstrated how our intuitions can influence our categorization of social behaviors by influencing which organism we think is the actor versus the recipient. The filial cannibalism case is similar, though slightly different. Here, even if we hold fixed who the actor is (the parent eating their offspring), there is still some ambiguity in classifying the behavior according to who the recipient is. Is it the offspring getting eaten? In that case the behavior is not altruistic, but selfish: The parent gains

---

[61] It is, however, common to appeal to kin selection to explain why filial cannibalism is less common than heterocannibalism, the eating of non-kin conspecifics (members of the same species that are not relatives) (Anthony, 2003, Dobler and Kölliker, 2009, Parsons et al., 2013).

[62] Whether offspring competition increases as relatedness increases needs further empirical investigation (Klug and Bonsall, 2007, p. 1345).

at the expense of the eaten offspring. Is the recipient the consumed's siblings? In that case, the behavior is altruistic: The parent sacrifices some of its current reproduction to benefit organisms it's highly related to (its offspring), similar to parental care. As discussed in Halperin and Levy (2022) and Section 2.3.2, it is likely best to treat these categorizations as heuristic rather than objective.

5.4 Broad-Scope Human Altruism

Although kin selection is a common explanation of altruism in nonhuman organisms, it is often dismissed fairly quickly when talking about broad-scope altruism in humans. It is argued that kin selection can only explain altruism toward immediate family members, and since what we are interested in explaining is widespread altruism toward non-kin, kin selection cannot be explanatorily helpful (see, e.g., Bowles and Gintis, 2011). Of course, humans also act altruistically toward kin, and generally more so. There are plenty of altruistic behaviors in humans that are discussed as examples of kin selection, ranging from classic examples like parental care to lifelong celibacy among Tibetan Buddhist monks, which leads to increased wealth and number of children for their brothers (Micheletti et al., 2022). While there are altruistic behaviors that generally only benefit kin, others are directed toward kin and non-kin alike, even strangers, with no expectation benefits being returned. That is, they are "broad-scope" (Birch, 2017b). It is likely that the explanation for kin-directed altruistic behaviors can proceed along different lines than the explanation for altruism toward non-kin, and would not necessarily need to appeal to anything besides kin selection.

This dismissal of kin selection for explaining broad-scope human altruism tends to be in response to a particular type of argument for the importance of kin selection, which is commonly referred to as the "big mistake hypothesis" (Henrich and Henrich, 2007, Bowles and Gintis, 2011, Tomasello et al., 2012, etc.). This hypothesis asserts that altruism evolved in humans at a time when we lived in small kin groups where, biologically, altruism was favored. In modern times, we are still altruistic because we have retained these genes for altruistic behavior even though they are no longer favored by evolution (see, e.g., Burnham and Johnson, 2005). This argument has become popularly known as the big mistake hypothesis because it implies that all our altruistic actions toward non-kin are just big mistakes – they are just misfirings of our desire to help kin in a world where we no longer primarily interact with kin.[63] However, the

---

[63] The big mistake hypothesis actually includes both misfirings due to desire to help kin and due to expectations of reciprocity, but we will focus on the kin selection part here.

response to this is that other primates can distinguish kin from non-kin, so we ought to expect the same of humans, and kin selection is unlikely to be important for explaining altruism in human societies because human groups were too large (and relatedness too low) at the time we think modern human society started to evolve (around the late Pleistocene) (Fehr and Henrich, 2003, Bowles and Gintis, 2011, p. 94-5).

Instead, group selection is proposed as the explanation of broad-scope altruism in modern humans.[64] Here is an example of how a group selection argument might proceed. The basic idea is that groups whose members are altruistic will tend to out-compete other groups because they will more often survive things like environmental crises or attack by a predator. While group selection is somewhat contentious as a type of biological evolution, it is often argued that it is more reasonable as a form of cultural evolution in human groups. This is because group selection requires variation between groups – for example, groups with various levels of altruists – and migration between groups tends to decrease this variation. While in nonhumans there is generally little to maintain this variation, in humans, culture can maintain group differences. In human groups, there are norms for how to behave. Forces like insider bias, the tendency to interact with people within one's own group, means that people tend to learn behaviors from within their own group. Additionally, conformist bias reduces within-group differences: Even if there is a fair bit of migration between groups, a group of altruists will remain a group of altruists because new members generally conform to the norms of the group. (See e.g., Okasha (2006, p. 159-60), Richerson and Boyd (2008, p. 162-3), and Bowles and Gintis (2011, p. 50-2) for further discussion.)

While not necessarily undermining the importance of group selection, some have offered up a way that kin selection may have been important in human evolutionary history, which does not fall prey to the same objections as the big mistake hypothesis. For example, we might note that even though genetic relatedness might have been low in human groups, *cultural* relatedness could still have been high (Birch, 2017b). The idea is that we can think of cultural traits as inherited (whether vertically, obliquely, or horizontally) and so in human groups people can be highly *culturally* related, even when there is low genetic relatedness. So, early humans would have tended to interact with others who had the same cultural trait – altruistic or not – even if they were not necessarily interacting with someone who had the same sort of genes. Therefore, we might

---

[64] Or, group selection in combination with some other factor, e.g., genetic evolution. Spelling out the details of these "gene-culture co-evolution" models is beyond the scope of this Element, but for details, see, e.g., Richerson and Boyd (1998, 1999, 2008).

appeal to a form of *cultural* kin selection in explaining human social behavior (Cavalli-Sforza and Feldman, 1981, Allison, 1992, Lehmann and Feldman, 2008, El Mouden et al., 2014, Birch, 2017b, Rubin, 2021).

Birch (2017b) argues for the potential importance of this selection process. In particular, he emphasizes the importance of horizontal transmission, where traits are transferred between individuals of the same generation, for human cultural evolution. He also argues for a diachronic conception of relatedness where one takes into account the (genetic or cultural) similarity between individuals not just at the time of interaction, but at other stages in their life cycle as well.[65] One particularly interesting claim that follows from this is that high relatedness should promote the evolution of altruism, even when it is only generated after the relevant interactions; a person can increase the reproductive output of others, then make it so that those others spread that social behavior.[66] The possibility of imitation after interaction is not something that is generally explored in models of cultural kin selection.

Let's take a simple example (from Rubin (2021)) to demonstrate how this might work.[67] We have people arranged on a "ring network" where everyone has two neighbors (i.e., everyone interacts with those directly next to them). This network choice is not meant to be realistic – humans would certainly have interacted with more than two others and there would be some form of clustering in the network – but there is no nonarbitrary way to divide agents into groups, which means that it is a high-K, low-G population (recall Section 4.2.2). In each round, or, time period, or generation, people do the following things: act (act altruistically and pay some cost to benefit neighbors, or do nothing), horizontal transfer (with some probability, adopt a cultural trait from a neighbor), and reproduce proportional to fitness. Then a new network is randomly formed with the offspring.[68]

In accord with Birch (2017b)'s framework, relatedness need not be high at the time the altruistic actions are performed; altruism can spread in a population even when horizontal transfer occurs only after an altruistic action has been

---

[65] Microbes are an interesting example of a case where genetic horizontal transfer is important. See Birch (2014b) and Birch (2017b), ch. 6.

[66] Note that cultural selection in the context of this model is best thought of as still tied to biological reproduction in that cultural traits influence reproductive success. This is what Birch (2017b, p. 197) calls *type-1 cultural selection*, or CS_1. Traits are passed on vertically from parents to offspring, though of course horizontal transmission also affects their evolution. This is opposed to CS_2, where traits affect cultural fitness (e.g., they influence the number of apprentices you have, who copy your behaviors, as opposed to your number of biological offspring).

[67] For the development of a general framework, in the context of the Price equation, see Birch (2017b), ch. 8.

[68] For further details of how the model works, see Rubin (2021).

performed. Since the network is randomly formed at the start of each round, there is no expected correlation between traits; relatedness is on average zero when the action is performed. This is true for both genetic and cultural relatedness. Instead, altruists confer a benefit on neighbors, who then (sometimes or often, depending on the likelihood of horizontal transfer) become altruists if they aren't already. So, the benefits are differentially conferred on individuals who are altruistic when it comes time to pass on the altruistic trait, if not at the time of the action. (Of course, we can also add in a stage of horizontal transfer before organisms act. The existence of horizontal transfer both before and after the organisms act generates higher relatedness and is more conducive to the evolution of altruism than just having transfer after.)

While this model is not very realistic, it does demonstrate the plausibility of the mechanism behind cultural kin selection. Additionally, this cultural kin selection explanation is compatible with the arguments that group selection was evolutionarily important to broad-scope human altruism. It could be that the benefits of such behavior are higher in one group than another, based on some ecological conditions, leading to altruism evolving in one group but not another. It also could be that there is more horizontal transmission occurring in one group than an other. In these cases, we would have groups with various levels of altruism, and then group selection could act on that variation among groups.

To quickly return to some of the questions discussed in Section 4, whether this model itself can be described as an example of group selection (where kin selection is thought of as a type of group selection) is debatable, even if we talk of trait groups and use the broad sense of group selection used by Wilson and Sober (1994), and Sober and Wilson (1999). A similar question arises for genetic models with a similar kind of continuous population structure. The answer seems to depend on the interpretation of the mathematical model. We can think of a spatial arrangement where an organism just produces some beneficial chemical where two others happen to be in range to make use of it. This might be possible to describe in terms of trait groups forming when one organism is in proximity to another, though this strikes me as a somewhat unnatural interpretation of the situation because, unlike in other examples, organisms don't group or pair up to interact, even temporarily.

6 Conclusion

The world is full of intriguing and perplexing social behavior. How are we to make sense of the evolutionary purpose of such things as filial cannibalism or eusociality? Here we have talked about some of the clarifying concepts and insightful explanations, as well as some confusions and debates surrounding the evolution of social behaviors.

There are a variety of different fitness concepts we may employ to capture how social behaviors affect the reproductive success of organisms that exhibit the behaviors and/or those with whom they interact. We have primarily focused on inclusive fitness, which has historically been seen as essential to the study of social evolution, but we have also discussed other fitness concepts along the way. There are also different selection processes we might argue are responsible for the evolution of social behavior. Here, we focused on kin selection but also discussed group selection. It is important to keep it straight that fitness and selection are different concepts within evolutionary theory. Nonetheless, these processes might each be connected in some kind of "natural" or "intuitive" way to different fitness calculations, which raises interesting questions about the epistemic gains of using different fitness concepts.

There are many questions left to address and much more work that can be fruitfully done. To round out this Element, I'll end with just three fairly broad topics of potential future research that have been touched on here. (Though, of course, there are always more!) First, there are questions remaining regarding our intuitions' impact on the categorization of behavior according to a four-part schema (Table 1, Sections 2.3.2 and 5.3). How much it matters for empirical practice that our categorizations are not totally objective is unclear; heuristic value might be fine in many or most experimental settings. However, it is certainly of theoretical importance, especially considering all the debates surrounding and effort that has gone into clarifying schemata for classification of social behavior (see, e.g., Wilson, 1979, 1990, West et al., 2007, Forber and Smead, 2015, Birch, 2017b).

There are also questions regarding whether (or when) inclusive fitness is a property of an individual, as described in Section 2.5. Furthermore, how does settling whether inclusive fitness is a property of an individual relate to its role in evolutionary theory, and the benefits we expect to gain from using inclusive, rather than some other concept of fitness, for example, if we want to think of an organism choosing its traits in order to maximize its (inclusive) fitness (Section 3.1.2) or according to a utility function described by inclusive fitness (Section 3.1.3)? What about if we want to think of inclusive fitness providing a stable criterion for improvement in an evolutionary process (Section 3.1.4)?

Finally, there are further connections to be made to philosophy of physics and further development needed for those connections already made here (mostly in Sections 3.2, 3.3, 4.3, and 5.2). For instance, what do we gain from reformulations of fitness, where we use different but equivalent calculations to describe evolutionary change, and how does this relate to claims that certain fitness calculations give us explanations that others do not (Sections 3.2 and 3.3)? What do the symmetries revealed by the relationship between inclusive and neighbor-modulated fitness, or inclusive and multilevel fitness, tell us about the empirical world (Sections 3.3 and 4.3)? Are there other reformulations in evolutionary theory, for example, other fitness concepts (Wagner, 2010, Huttegger et al., 2021) or between different evolutionary dynamics (Page and Nowak, 2002), that reveal interesting or important epistemic dependence relations (Sections 3.3)? Is the relationship between kin and group selection one where we want to say one of those process is more "fundamental" and, if so, what do we mean by "fundamental" (Section 4.3)? There is fertile ground here yet to be explored.

References

P. Abbot, J. Abe, J. Alcock, and et al. Inclusive fitness theory and eusociality. *Nature*, 471:E1–E4, 2011.

E. Akçay and J. Van Cleve. There is no fitness but fitness, and the lineage is its bearer. *Philosophical Transactions of the Royal Society B: Biological Sciences*, 371(1687):20150085, 2016.

B. Allen and M. A. Nowak. There is no inclusive fitness at the level of the individual. *Current Opinion in Behavioral Sciences*, 12:122–128, 2016.

B. Allen, M. A. Nowak, and E. O. Wilson. Limitations of inclusive fitness. *Proceedings of the National Academy of Sciences*, 110:20135–20139, 2013.

P. D. Allison. Cultural relatedness under oblique and horizontal transmission rules. *Ethology and Sociobiology*, 13(3):153–169, 1992.

C. Anderson and N. R. Franks. Teams in animal societies. *Behavioral Ecology*, 12(5):534–540, 2001.

C. Anderson and D. W. McShea. Individual versus social complexity, with particular reference to ant colonies. *Biological Reviews*, 76(2):211–237, 2001.

C. Anderson, N. R. Franks, and D. W. McShea. The complexity and hierarchical structure of tasks in insect societies. *Animal Behaviour*, 62(4):643–651, 2001.

C. D. Anthony. Kinship influences cannibalism in the wolf spider, pardosa milvina. *Journal of Insect Behavior*, 16(1):23–36, 2003.

M. Archetti. The volunteer's dilemma and the optimal size of a social group. *Journal of Theoretical Biology*, 261:475–480, 2009a.

M. Archetti. Cooperation and the volunteer's dilemma and the strategy of conflict in public goods games. *Journal of Evolutionary Biology*, 22:2129–2200, 2009b.

R. Axelrod and W. D. Hamilton. The evolution of cooperation. *Science*, 211(4489):1390–1396, 1981.

J.-C. Belles-Isles and G. FitzGerald. Filial cannibalism in sticklebacks: A reproductive management strategy? *Ethology Ecology & Evolution*, 3(1):49–62, 1991.

J. Birch. Hamilton's rule and its discontents. *British Journal for the Philosophy of Science*, 65(2):381–411, 2014a.

J. Birch. Gene mobility and the concept of relatedness. *Biology & Philosophy*, 29(4):445–476, 2014b.

J. Birch. Hamilton's two conceptions of social fitness. *Philosophy of Science*, 83(5):848–860, 2016.

J. Birch. The inclusive fitness controversy: Finding a way forward. *Royal Society Open Science*, 4(7):170335, 2017a.

J. Birch. *The Philosophy of Social Evolution*. Oxford University Press, 2017b.

J. Birch. Inclusive fitness as a criterion for improvement. *Studies in History and Philosophy of Science Part C: Studies in History and Philosophy of Biological and Biomedical Sciences*, 76:101186, 2019a.

J. Birch. Are kin and group selection rivals or friends? *Current Biology*, 29(11):R433–R438, 2019b.

J. Birch. Kin selection, group selection, and the varieties of population structure. *The British Journal for the Philosophy of Science*, 71:259–286, 2020.

J. Birch and J. A. Marshall. Queller's separation condition explained and defended. *The American Naturalist*, 184(4):531–540, 2014.

J. Birch and S. Okasha. Kin selection and its critics. *BioScience*, 65(6):22–32, 2015.

A. P. Bose. Parent–offspring cannibalism throughout the animal kingdom: A review of adaptive hypotheses. *Biological Reviews*, 97(5):1868–1885, 2022.

A. F. Bourke. Genetics, relatedness and social behaviour in insect societies. In *Symposium-Royal Entomological Society of London*, volume 22, page 1, 2005.

S. Bowles and H. Gintis. *A Cooperative Species: Human Reciprocity and Its Evolution*. Princeton University Press, 2011.

K. Brading and E. Castellani. *Symmetries in Physics: Philosophical Reflections*. Cambridge University Press, 2003.

Y. Brandvain, J. Van Cleve, F. Ubeda, and J. F. Wilkins. Demography, kinship, and the evolving theory of genomic imprinting. *Trends in Genetics*, 27(7):251–257, 2011.

J. P. Bruner and H. Rubin. Inclusive fitness and the problem of honest communication. *The British Journal for the Philosophy of Science*, 71(1):115–137, 2020.

H. Burda, R. L. Honeycutt, S. Begall, O. Locker-Grütjen, and A. Scharff. Are naked and common mole-rats eusocial and if so, why? *Behavioral Ecology and Sociobiology*, 47(5):293–303, 2000.

T. C. Burnham and D. D. Johnson. The biological and evolutionary logic of human cooperation. *Analyse & Kritik*, 27(1):113–135, 2005.

K. Burns, I. Hutton, and L. Shepherd. Primitive eusociality in a land plant? *Ecology*, 102(9):e03373, 2021.

B. Calcott. The other cooperation problem: Generating benefit. *Biology & Philosophy*, 23(2):179–203, 2008.

L. L. Cavalli-Sforza and M. W. Feldman. *Cultural Transmission and Evolution: A Quantitative Approach*. Princeton University Press, 1981.

M. Chapuisat and L. Keller. Testing kin selection with sex allocation data in eusocial hymenoptera. *Heredity*, 82(5):473–478, 1999.

E. Clarke. The multiple realizability of biological individuals. *The Journal of Philosophy*, 110(8):413–435, 2013.

S. Creel. How to measure inclusive fitness. *Proceedings of the Royal Society of London. Series B: Biological Sciences*, 241(1302):229–231, 1990.

R. Dawkins. *The Selfish Gene*. Oxford University Press, 1976.

R. Dawkins. Replicator selection and the extended phenotype 3. *Zeitschrift für Tierpsychologie*, 47(1):61–76, 1978.

R. Dobler and M. Kölliker. Kin-selected siblicide and cannibalism in the European earwig. *Behavioral Ecology*, 21(2):257–263, 2009. https://doi.org/10.1093/beheco/arp184.

J. E. Duffy, C. L. Morrison, and Rubén Ríos. Multiple origins of eusociality among sponge-dwelling shrimps (synalpheus). *Evolution*, 54(2):503–516, 2000.

C. El Mouden, J.-B. André, O. Morin, and D. Nettle. Cultural transmission and the evolution of human behaviour: A general approach based on the price equation. *Journal of Evolutionary Biology*, 27(2):231–241, 2014.

I. Eshel. On the changing concept of evolutionary population stability as a reflection of a changing point of view in the quantitative theory of evolution. *Journal of Mathematical Biology*, 34(5):485–510, 1996.

I. Eshel and M. W. Feldman. Optimality and evolutionary stability under short-term and long-term selection. *Adaptationism and Optimality*, 161–190, 2001.

S. Feferman. Mathematical intuition vs. mathematical monsters. *Synthese*, 125(3):317–332, 2000.

E. Fehr and J. Henrich. Is strong reciprocity a maladaptation? On the evolutionary foundations of human altruism. In P. Hammerstein, editor, *Mathematical Evolutionary Theory*, pages 55–82. MIT Press, 2003.

R. A. Fisher. *The Genetical Theory of Natural Selection*. Oxford University Press, 1930.

R. M. Fisher, C. K. Cornwallis, and S. A. West. Group formation, relatedness, and the evolution of multicellularity. *Current Biology*, 23(12):1120–1125, 2013.

G. J. FitzGerald. Filial cannibalism in fishes: Why do parents eat their offspring? *Trends in Ecology & Evolution*, 7(1):7–10, 1992.

D. J. Fletcher, C. D. Michener. *Kin Recognition in Animals*. John Wiley, 1987.

P. Forber and R. Smead. The evolution of fairness through spite. *Proceedings of the Royal Society B: Biological Sciences*, 281(1780):20132439, 2014.

P. Forber and R. Smead. Evolution and the classification of social behavior. *Biology & Philosophy*, 30:405–421, 2015.

S. Fortunato. Community detection in graphs. *Physics Reports*, 486(3-5):75–174, 2010.

S. Frank. *Foundations of Social Evolution*. Princeton University Press, 1998.

S. Frank. Natural selection. vii. history and interpretation of kin selection theory. *Journal of Evolutionary Biology*, 26:1151–1184, 2013.

L. Fromhage and M. D. Jennions. The strategic reference gene: An organismal theory of inclusive fitness. *Proceedings of the Royal Society B*, 286(1904):20190459, 2019.

Z. Fulker, P. Forber, R. Smead, and C. Riedl. Spite is contagious in dynamic networks. *Nature Communications*, 12(1):1–9, 2021.

R. Gadagkar. Ant, bee and wasp social evolution. In J. C. Choe, editor, *Encyclopedia of Animal Behavior (2nd ed.)*, pages 599–608. Academic Press, 2nd ed., 2019. ISBN 978-0-12-813252-4. https://doi.org/10.1016/B978-0-12-809633-8.90136-5. www.sciencedirect.com/science/article/pii/B9780128096338901365.

J. Garay, Z. Varga, M. Gámez, and T. Cabello. Sib cannibalism can be adaptive for kin. *Ecological Modelling*, 334:51–59, 2016.

A. Gardner. Adaptation as organism design. *Biology Letters*, 5(6):861–864, 2009.

A. Gardner. The genetical theory of multilevel selection. *Journal of Evolutionary Biology*, 28(2):305–319, 2015.

P. Godfrey-Smith. Local interaction, multilevel selection, and evolutionary transitions. *Biological Theory*, 1(4):372–380, 2006.

P. Godfrey-Smith. Varieties of population structure and the levels of selection. *The British Journal for the Philosophy of Science*, 59(1):25–50, 2008.

P. Godfrey-Smith. *Darwinian Populations and Natural Selection*. Oxford University Press, 2009.

A. Grafen. The hawk-dove game played between relatives. *Animal Behaviour*, 27:905–907, 1979.

A. Grafen. How not to measure inclusive fitness. *Nature*, 298(29):425–426, 1982.

A. Grafen. Natural selection, kin selection and group selection. *Behavioural Ecology: An Evolutionary Approach*, 2:62–84, 1984a.

A. Grafen. Natural selection, kin selection and group selection. In J. Krebs and N. Davies, editors, *Behavioural Ecology*. pages 62–84, Blackwell Scientific, 2nd ed., 1984b.

A. Grafen. A geometric view of relatedness. *Oxford Surveys in Evolutionary Biology*, 2(2):28–89, 1985.

A. Grafen. Split sex ratios and the evolutionary origins of eusociality. *Journal of Theoretical Biology*, 122(1):95–121, 1986.

A. Grafen. Optimization of inclusive fitness. *Journal of Theoretical Biology*, 238(3):541–563, 2006.

A. Grafen. The simplest formal argument for fitness optimization. *Journal of Genetics*, 87(4):421–433, 2008.

A. Grafen. Formalizing darwinism and inclusive fitness theory. *Philosophical Transactions of the Royal Society of London B: Biological Sciences*, 364(1533):3135–3141, 2009.

H. Greaves and D. Wallace. Empirical consequences of symmetries. *The British Journal for the Philosophy of Science*, 65:59–89, 2014.

A. S. Griffin and S. A. West. Kin discrimination and the benefit of helping in cooperatively breeding vertebrates. *Science*, 302(5645):634–636, 2003.

A. S. Griffin, S. A. West, and A. Buckling. Cooperation and competition in pathogenic bacteria. *Nature*, 430(7003):1024–1027, 2004.

H. Hahn. The crisis in intuition. In Brian McGuinness, editor, *Empiricism, Logic and Mathematics*, pages 73–102. The Netherlands: Springer, 1980.

D. Haig. Parental antagonism, relatedness asymmetries, and genomic imprinting. *Proceedings of the Royal Society of London. Series B: Biological Sciences*, 264(1388):1657–1662, 1997.

D. Haig. Genomic imprinting, sex-biased dispersal, and social behavior. *Annals of the New York Academy of Sciences*, 907(1):149–163, 2000a.

D. Haig. The kinship theory of genomic imprinting. *Annual Review of Ecology and Systematics*, 31:9–32, 2000b.

D. Haig. *Genomic Imprinting and Kinship*. Rutgers University Press, 2002.

D. Haig. Troubled sleepnight waking, breastfeeding and parent–offspring conflict. *Evolution, Medicine, and Public Health*, 2014(1):32–39, 2014.

D. Haig and R. Wharton. Prader-willi syndrome and the evolution of human childhood. *American Journal of Human Biology*, 15(3):320–329, 2003.

T. Halperin and A. Levy. What, if anything, is biological altruism? *British Journal for the Philosophy of Science*, 2022. https://doi.org/10.1086/716097.

W. D. Hamilton. The genetical evolution of social behavior i and ii. *Journal of Theoretical Biology*, 7:1–16, 1964.

W. D. Hamilton. Selfish and spiteful behaviour in an evolutionary model. *Nature*, 228(5277):1218–1220, 1970.

W. D. Hamilton. Altruism and related phenomena, mainly in social insects. *Annual Review of Ecology and Systematics*, 3:193–232, 1972.

W. D. Hamilton. Innate social aptitudes of man: An approach from evolutionary genetics. *Biosocial Anthropology*, 133:315–352, 1975.

W. D. Hamilton and R. M. May. Dispersal in stable habitats. *Nature*, 269(5629):578–581, 1977.

P. Hammerstein. Streetcar theory and long-term evolution. *Science*, 273(5278):1032–1032, 1996.

P. Hammerstein and R. Selten. Game theory and evolutionary biology. *Handbook of Game Theory with Economic Applications*, 2:929–993, 1994.

J. Henrich. Cultural group selection, coevolutionary processes and large-scale cooperation. *Journal of Economic Behavior & Organization*, 53(1):3–35, 2004.

N. Henrich and J. P. Henrich. *Why Humans Cooperate: A Cultural and Evolutionary Explanation*. Oxford University Press, 2007.

E. Heydon. Exploring an evolutionary paradox: An analysis of the "spite effect" and the "nearly neutral effect" in synergistic models of finite populations. *Philosophy of Science*, 2023.

W. G. S. Hines and J. Maynard Smith. Games between relatives. *Journal of Theoretical Biology*, 79(1):19–30, 1979.

S. B. Hrdy. Infanticide as a primate reproductive strategy: Conflict is basic to all creatures that reproduce sexually, because the genotypes, and hence self-interests, of consorts are necessarily nonidentical. Infanticide among langurs illustrates an extreme form of this conflict. *American Scientist*, 65(1):40–49, 1977.

S. B. Hrdy. Infanticide among animals: A review, classification, and examination of the implications for the reproductive strategies of females. *Ethology and Sociobiology*, 1(1):13–40, 1979.

D. L. Hull. Individuality and selection. *Annual Review of Ecology and Systematics*, 11:311–332, 1980.

J. Hunt. Understanding and equivalent reformulations. *Philosophy of Science*, 88(5):810–823, 2021a.

J. Hunt. Epistemic dependence & understanding: Reformulating through symmetry. *British Journal for the Philosophy of Science*, 2021b.

J. Hunt. *Symmetry and Reformulation: On Intellectual Progress in Science and Mathematics*. PhD Thesis, University of Michigan, 2022.

J. H. Hunt. Trait mapping and salience in the evolution of eusocial vespid wasps. *Evolution*, 53(1):225–237, 1999.

S. M. Huttegger, H. Rubin, and K. J. Zollman. Invariance and symmetry in evolutionary dynamics. *American Philosophical Quarterly*, 58(1):63–78, 2021.

E. Jablonka and M. J. Lamb. *Evolution in Four Dimensions, Revised Edition: Genetic, Epigenetic, Behavioral, and Symbolic Variation in the History of Life*. MIT Press, 2014.

K. Jensen. Punishment and spite, the dark side of cooperation. *Philosophical Transactions of the Royal Society B: Biological Sciences*, 365(1553):2635–2650, 2010.

R. Johnstone. Efficacy and honesty in communication between relatives. *The American Naturalist*, 152:45–58, 1998.

R. Johnstone and A. Grafen. The continuous Sir Philip Sidney game: A simple model of biological signaling. *Journal of Theoretical Biology*, 156:215–234, 1992.

P. Kennedy and A. N. Radford. Sibling quality and the haplodiploidy hypothesis. *Biology Letters*, 16(3):20190764, 2020.

H. Klug and M. B. Bonsall. When to care for, abandon, or eat your offspring: The evolution of parental care and filial cannibalism. *The American Naturalist*, 170(6):886–901, 2007.

H. Klug, K. Lindströum, and C. M. S. Mary. Parents benefit from eating offspring: Density-dependent egg survivorship compensates for filial cannibalism. *Evolution*, 60(10):2087–2095, 2006.

V. Koliofotis and P. Verreault-Julien. Hamilton's rule: A non-causal explanation? *Studies in History and Philosophy of Science*, 92:109–118, 2022.

T. Krama, J. Vrublevska, T. M. Freeberg et al. You mob my owl, I'll mob yours: Birds play tit-for-tat game. *Scientific Reports*, 2(1):1–3, 2012.

J. J. Lee and C. C. Chow. The causal meaning of Fisher's average effect. *Genetics Research*, 95(2–3):89–109, 2013.

L. Lehmann and M. W. Feldman. The co-evolution of culturally inherited altruistic helping and cultural transmission under random group formation. *Theoretical Population Biology*, 73(4):506–516, 2008.

L. Lehmann and F. Rousset. The genetical theory of social behaviour. *Philosophical Transactions of the Royal Society B: Biological Sciences*, 369(1642):20130357, 2014.

L. Lehmann, L. Keller, S. West, and D. Roze. Group selection and kin selection: Two concepts but one process. *Proceedings of the National Academy of Sciences*, 104(16):6736–6739, 2007.

S. R. Levin and A. Grafen. Inclusive fitness is an indispensable approximation for understanding organismal design. *Evolution*, 73(6):1066–1076, 2019.

S. R. Levin and A. Grafen. Extending the range of additivity in using inclusive fitness. *Ecology and Evolution*, 11(5):1970–1983, 2021.

T. Lewens. Neo-paleyan biology. *Studies in History and Philosophy of Science Part C: Studies in History and Philosophy of Biological and Biomedical Sciences*, 76:101185, 2019.

X. Liao, S. Rong, and D. C. Queller. Relatedness, conflict, and the evolution of eusociality. *PLoS Biology*, 13(3):e1002098, 2015.

E. Lloyd. Units and levels of selection: An anatomy of the units of selection debate. In R. Singh, C. Krimbas, D. Paul, and J. Beatty, editors, *Thinking about Evolution*. Cambridge University Press, pages 267–291, 2001.

E. Lloyd. Units and levels of selection. *Stanford Encyclopedia of Philosophy*, 2017.

A. Manica. Filial cannibalism in teleost fish. *Biological Reviews*, 77(2):261–277, 2002.

P. Marrow, R. A. Johnstone, and L. D. Hurst. Riding the evolutionary streetcar: Where population genetics and game theory meet. *Trends in Ecology & Evolution*, 11(11):445–446, 1996.

J. A. Marshall. Queller's rule ok: Comment on van Veelen "when inclusive fitness if right and when it can be wrong." *Journal of Theoretical Biology*, 270:185–188, 2011.

J. A. Marshall. *Social Evolution and Inclusive Fitness Theory*. Princeton University Press, 2015.

J. M. Mateo. Kin-recognition abilities and nepotism as a function of sociality. *Proceedings of the Royal Society of London. Series B: Biological Sciences*, 269(1492):721–727, 2002.

M. Matthen and A. Ariew. Two ways of thinking about fitness and natural selection. *The Journal of Philosophy*, 99(2):55–83, 2002.

J. Maynard Smith. Group selection and kin selection. *Nature*, 201(4924):1145–1147, 1964.

J. Maynard Smith. Group selection. *The Quarterly Review of Biology*, 51(2):277–283, 1976.

J. Maynard Smith. Optimization theory in evolution. *Annual Review of Ecology and Systematics*, 9:31–56, 1978.

J. Maynard Smith. Models of evolution. *Proceedings of the Royal Society of London. Series B. Biological Sciences*, 219(1216):315–325, 1983.

J. Maynard Smith. Evolutionary Progress and Levels of Selection. In: Nitecki M.H. (ed.), Evolutionary Progress, Chicago: University of Chicago Press, pp. 219–230.

J. Maynard Smith. Honest signaling, the Philip Sidney game. *Animal Behavior*, 42:1034–1035, 1991.

J. Maynard Smith. The origin of altruism. *Nature*, 393(6686):639–640, 1998.

N. J. Mehdiabadi, H. K. Reeve, and U. G. Mueller. Queens versus workers: Sex-ratio conflict in eusocial hymenoptera. *Trends in Ecology & Evolution*, 18(2):88–93, 2003.

A. Mesoudi, A. Whiten, and K. N. Laland. Towards a unified science of cultural evolution. *Behavioral and Brain Sciences*, 29(4):329–347, 2006.

J. Meunier, S. A. West, and M. Chapuisat. Split sex ratios in the social hymenoptera: A meta-analysis. *Behavioral Ecology*, 19(2):382–390, 2008.

A. J. Micheletti, E. Ge, L. Zhou et al. Religious celibacy brings inclusive fitness benefits. *Proceedings of the Royal Society B*, 289(1977):20220965, 2022.

R. E. Michod. *Darwinian Dynamics: Evolutionary Transitions in Fitness and Individuality*. Princeton University Press, 2000.

A. Mochizuki, Y. Takeda, and Y. Iwasa. The evolution of genomic imprinting. *Genetics*, 144(3):1283–1295, 1996.

S. Murgueitio Ramírez. A puzzle concerning local symmetries and their empirical significance. *The British Journal for the Philosophy of Science*, 73:1021–1044, 2020.

M. Nowak and K. Sigmund. The evolution of stochastic strategies in the prisoner's dilemma. *Acta Applicandae Mathematicae*, 20(3):247–265, 1990.

M. A. Nowak. Five rules for the evolution of cooperation. *Science*, 314(5805):1560–1563, 2006.

M. A. Nowak, C. E. Tarnita, and E. O. Wilson. The evolution of eusociality. *Nature*, 466(26):1057–1062, 2010.

M. A. Nowak, C. E. Tarnita, and E. O. Wilson. Nowak el al. reply. *Nature*, 471:E9–E10, 2011.

S. Okasha. Why won't the group selection controversy go away? *British Journal for the Philosophy of Science*, 52(1), 2001.

S. Okasha. Genetic relatedness and the evolution of altruism. *Philosophy of Science*, 69(1):138–149, 2002.

S. Okasha. *Evolution and the Levels of Selection*. Oxford University Press, 2006.

S. Okasha. *Agents and Goals in Evolution*. Oxford University Press, 2018.

S. Okasha. The relation between kin and multilevel selection: An approach using causal graphs. *The British Journal for the Philosophy of Science*, 67:435–470, 2020.

S. Okasha and J. Martens. The causal meaning of Hamilton's rule. *Royal Society Open Science*, 3(3):160037, 2016a.

S. Okasha and J. Martens. Hamilton's rule, inclusive fitness maximization, and the goal of individual behaviour in symmetric two-player games. *Journal of Evolutionary Biology*, 29:473–482, 2016b.

S. Okasha and C. Paternotte. Group adaptation, formal darwinism and contextual analysis. *Journal of Evolutionary Biology*, 25(6):1127–1139, 2012.

S. Okasha, J. A. Weymark, and W. Bossert. Inclusive fitness maximization: An axiomatic approach. *Journal of Theoretical Biology*, 350:24–31, 2014.

M. Orlove and C. L. Wood. Coefficients of relationship and coefficients of relatedness in kin selection: A covariance form for the rho formula. *Journal of Theoretical Biology*, 73(4):679–686, 1978.

J. Otsuka. *The Role of Mathematics in Evolutionary Theory*. Cambridge University Press, 2019.

K. M. Page and M. A. Nowak. Unifying evolutionary dynamics. *Journal of Theoretical Biology*, 219(1):93–98, 2002.

W. Parsons, W. Zhong, and V. H. Rudolf. Mating status and kin recognition influence the strength of cannibalism. *Animal Behaviour*, 85(2):365–369, 2013.

M. Patten, L. Ross, J. Curley et al. The evolution of genomic imprinting: Theories, predictions and empirical tests. *Heredity*, 113(2):119–128, 2014.

G. A. Polis. The evolution and dynamics of intraspecific predation. *Annual Review of Ecology and Systematics*, 12:225–251, 1981.

C. Prescod-Weinstein. *The Disordered Cosmos: A Journey into Dark Matter, Spacetime, and Dreams Deferred*. Hachett, 2021.

D. Queller. What life is for: A commentary on Fromhage and Jennions. *Proceedings of the Royal Society B*, 286(1905):20191060, 2019.

D. C. Queller. A general model for kin selection. *Evolution*, 46(2):376–380, 1992a.

D. C. Queller. Quantitative genetics, inclusive fitness, and group selection. *The American Naturalist*, 139(3):540–558, 1992b.

D. C. Queller. The measurement and meaning of inclusive fitness. *Animal Behaviour*, 51(1):229–232, 1996.

D. C. Queller. Theory of genomic imprinting conflict in social insects. *BMC Evolutionary Biology*, 3(1):1–23, 2003.

D. C. Queller. Expanded social fitness and Hamilton's rule for kin, kith, and kind. *Proceedings of the National Academy of Sciences*, 108(Supplement 2):10792–10799, 2011.

D. C. Queller. The gene's eye view, the Gouldian knot, Fisherian swords and the causes of selection. *Philosophical Transactions of the Royal Society B*, 375(1797):20190354, 2020.

D. C. Queller and J. E. Strassmann. Kin selection and social insects. *BioScience*, 48(3):165–175, 1998.

D. C. Queller and J. E. Strassmann. Beyond society: The evolution of organismality. *Philosophical Transactions of the Royal Society B: Biological Sciences*, 364(1533):3143–3155, 2009.

P. Rautiala, H. Helanterä, and M. Puurtinen. Extended haplodiploidy hypothesis. *Evolution Letters*, 3(3):263–270, 2019.

P. J. Richerson and R. Boyd. The evolution of human ultra-sociality. *Indoctrinability, Ideology, and Warfare: Evolutionary Perspectives*, In: Eibl-Eibesfeldt and F. Salter, Berghahn Books. 71–95, 1998.

P. J. Richerson and R. Boyd. Complex societies: The evolutionary origins of a crude superorganism. *Human Nature*, 10:253–289, 1999.

P. J. Richerson and R. Boyd. *Not By Genes Alone: How Culture Transformed Human Evolution*. University of Chicago Press, 2008.

D. Rickles. A philosopher looks at string dualities. *Studies in History and Philosophy of Science Part B: Studies in History and Philosophy of Modern Physics*, 42(1):54–67, 2011.

A. M. Rodrigues and A. Gardner. Inclusive fitness: A scientific revolution. In Thomas E. Dickins, Benjamin J.A. Dickins, editor, *Evolutionary Biology: Contemporary and Historical Reflections upon Core Theory*, pages 343–360. Springer, 2023.

A. Rosas. Beyond inclusive fitness? On a simple and general explanation for the evolution of altruism. *Philosophy & Theory in Biology*, 2:1–9, 2010.

S. Rosenstock, T. W. Barrett, and J. O. Weatherall. On Einstein algebras and relativistic spacetimes. *Studies in History and Philosophy of Science Part B: Studies in History and Philosophy of Modern Physics*, 52:309–316, 2015.

L. Ross, A. Gardner, N. Hardy, and S. A. West. Ecology, not the genetics of sex determination, determines who helps in eusocial populations. *Current Biology*, 23(23):2383–2387, 2013.

F. Rousset. Inbreeding and relatedness coefficients: What do they measure? *Heredity*, 88:371–380, 2002.

H. Rubin. Genetic models in evolutionary game theory: The evolution of altruism. *Erkenntnis*, 80(6):1175–1189, 2015.

H. Rubin. The phenotypic gambit: Selective pressures and ESS methodology in evolutionary game theory. *Biology & Philosophy*, 31(4):551–569, 2016.

H. Rubin. The debate over inclusive fitness as a debate over methodologies. *Philosophy of Science*, 85(1):1–30, 2018.

H. Rubin. Reintroducing kin selection to the human behavioral sciences. *Philosophy of Science*, 88(1):44–66, 2021.

H. Rubin. Unlike agents: The role of correlation in economics and biology. In A. du Crest, M. Valkovic, A. Ariew, H. Desmond, P. Huneman, and

T. Reydon, editors, *Evolutionary Thinking across Disciplines: Problems and Perspectives in Generalized Darwinism*. Synthese, 375–397, 2023.

E. Sampaio, M. C. Seco, R. Rosa, and S. Gingins. Octopuses punch fishes during collaborative interspecific hunting events. *Ecology*, 102(3):1–4, 2021.

A. Shavit and R. L. Millstein. Group selection is dead! Long live group selection? *BioScience*, 58(7):574–575, 2008.

C. Simonet and L. McNally. Kin selection explains the evolution of cooperation in the gut microbiota. *Proceedings of the National Academy of Sciences*, 118(6):e2016046118, 2021.

B. Skyrms. Altruism, inclusive fitness, and the logic of decision. *Philosophy of Science*, 69:S104–S111, 2002.

R. Smead and P. Forber. The evolutionary dynamics of spite in finite populations. *Evolution: International Journal of Organic Evolution*, 67(3):698–707, 2013.

E. Sober and D. S. Wilson. *Unto Others: The Evolution and Psychology of Unselfish Behavior*. Harvard University Press, 1999.

P. Spirtes, C. N. Glymour, R. Scheines, and D. Heckerman. *Causation, Prediction, and Search*. MIT Press, 2000.

P. T. Starks. Recognition systems: From components to conservation. In *Annales Zoologici Fennici*, volume 41, pages 689–690. Helsinki: Suomen Biologian Seura Vanamo, 1964–, 2004.

S. Stephens. The genetics of "corky" ii. further studies on its genetic basis in relation to the general problem of interspecific isolating mechanisms. *Journal of Genetics*, 50:9–20, 1950.

J. E. Strassmann, R. E. Page, G. E. Robinson, and T. D. Seeley. Kin selection and eusociality. *Nature*, 471(7339):E5–E6, 2011.

C. Taylor and M. A. Nowak. Transforming the dilemma. *Evolution*, 61(10):2281–2292, 2007.

G. Taylor, P. D. Wild and A. Gardner. Direct fitness or inclusive fitness: How shall we model kin selection? *Journal of Evolutionary Biology*, 20:301–309, 2007.

B. L. Thorne. Evolution of eusociality in termites. *Annual Review of Ecology and Systematics*, 28:27–54, 1997.

M. Tomasello, A. P. Melis, C. Tennie, E. Wyman, and E. Herrmann. Two key steps in the evolution of human cooperation. *Current Anthropology*, 53(6):673–692, 2012.

R. Trivers. *Social Evolution*. Benjamin/Cummings, 1985.

R. L. Trivers. The evolution of reciprocal altruism. *The Quarterly Review of Biology*, 46(1):35–57, 1971.

R. L. Trivers and H. Hare. Haploidploidy and the evolution of the social insect: The unusual traits of the social insects are uniquely explained by Hamilton's kinship theory. *Science*, 191(4224):249–263, 1976.

F. Úbeda and A. Gardner. A model for genomic imprinting in the social brain: Adults. *Evolution: International Journal of Organic Evolution*, 65(2):462–475, 2011.

J. Van Cleve, M. W. Feldman, and L. Lehmann. How demography, life history, and kinship shape the evolution of genomic imprinting. *The American Naturalist*, 176(4):440–455, 2010.

M. van Veelen. On the use of the Price equation. *Journal of Theoretical Biology*, 237:412–426, 2005.

M. van Veelen. Group selection, kin selection, altruism and cooperation: When inclusive fitness is right and when it can be wrong. *Journal of Theoretical Biology*, 259(3):589–600, 2009.

M. van Veelen. The replicator dynamics with n players and population structure. *Journal of Theoretical Biology*, 276(1):78–85, 2011a.

M. van Veelen. A rule is not a rule if it changes from case to case (a reply to Marshall's comment). *Journal of Theoretical Biology*, 270(1):189–195, 2011b.

M. van Veelen, J. García, M. W. Sabelis, and M. Egas. Group selection and inclusive fitness are not equivalent; the Price equation vs. models and statistics. *Journal of Theoretical Biology*, 299:64–80, 2012.

M. van Veelen, S. Luo, and B. Simon. A simple model of group selection that cannot be analyzed with inclusive fitness. *Journal of Theoretical Biology*, 360:279–289, 2014.

R. Ventura. The evolution of cooperation in finite populations with synergistic payoffs. *Biology & Philosophy*, 34(4):1–13, 2019.

M. J. Wade. A critical review of the models of group selection. *The Quarterly Review of Biology*, 53(2):101–114, 1978.

M. J. Wade. Soft selection, hard selection, kin selection, and group selection. *The American Naturalist*, 125(1):61–73, 1985.

G. P. Wagner. The measurement theory of fitness. *Evolution: International Journal of Organic Evolution*, 64(5):1358–1376, 2010.

D. M. Walsh, A. Ariew, and M. Matthen. Four pillars of statisticalism. *Philosophy, Theory, and Practice in Biology*, 9(1):1–18, 2017.

J. O. Weatherall. Part 1: Theoretical equivalence in physics. *Philosophy Compass*, 14(5):e12592, 2019.

S. A. West and A. Gardner. Adaptation and inclusive fitness. *Current Biology*, 23(13):R577–R584, 2013.

S. A. West, A. S. Griffin, and A. Gardner. Social semantics: Altruism, cooperation, mutualism, strong reciprocity and group selection. *Journal of Evolutionary Biology*, 20(2):415–432, 2007.

S. A. West, A. S. Griffin, and A. Gardner. Social semantics: How useful has group selection been? *Journal of Evolutionary Biology*, 21(1):374–385, 2008.

S. A. West, C. El Mouden, and A. Gardner. Sixteen common misconceptions about the evolution of cooperation in humans. *Evolution and Human Behavior*, 32(4):231–262, 2011.

M. J. West Eberhard. The evolution of social behavior by kin selection. *The Quarterly Review of Biology*, 50(1):1–33, 1975.

D. E. Wheeler. Developmental and physiological determinants of caste in social hymenoptera: Evolutionary implications. *The American Naturalist*, 128(1):13–34, 1986.

G. Wild and A. Traulsen. The different limits of weak selection and the evolutionary dynamics of finite populations. *Journal of Theoretical Biology*, 247(2):382–390, 2007.

G. C. Williams. A defense of reductionism in evolutionary biology. *Oxford Surveys in Evolutionary Biology*, 2:1–27, 1985.

D. S. Wilson. A theory of group selection. *Proceedings of the National Academy of Sciences*, 72(1):143–146, 1975.

D. S. Wilson. Structured demes and trait-group variation. *The American Naturalist*, 113(4):606–610, 1979.

D. S. Wilson. Weak altruism, strong group selection. *Oikos*, 59:135–140, 1990.

D. S. Wilson and E. Sober. Reintroducing group selection to the human behavioral sciences. *Behavioral and Brain Sciences*, 17(4):585–608, 1994.

E. O. Wilson. One giant leap: How insects achieved altruism and colonial life. *BioScience*, 58(1):17–25, 2008.

P. J. Woodford. The many meanings of "cost" and "benefit": Biological altruism, biological agency, and the identification of social behaviours. *Biology & Philosophy*, 34(1):1–22, 2019.

J. Wu and J. Weatherall. Between a stone and a Hausdorff space. *The British Journal for the Philosophy of Science*, 0(ja):null, 2024. https://doi.org/10.1086/728532. www.journals.uchicago.edu/doi/abs/10.1086/728532.

Acknowledgments

Thanks to Karthik Panchanathan, Mike Schneider, and two anonymous reviewers for very helpful comments. Thanks also to the several philosophers of physics who took the time to talk to me about fundamentality, equivalence, and other ideas related to Sections 3.2 and 4.3. (See footnote 44.)

Cambridge Elements

Philosophy of Biology

Grant Ramsey
KU Leuven

Grant Ramsey is a BOFZAP research professor at the Institute of Philosophy, KU Leuven, Belgium. His work centers on philosophical problems at the foundation of evolutionary biology. He has been awarded the Popper Prize twice for his work in this area. He also publishes in the philosophy of animal behavior, human nature and the moral emotions. He runs the Ramsey Lab (theramseylab.org), a highly collaborative research group focused on issues in the philosophy of the life sciences.

Michael Ruse
Florida State University

Michael Ruse is the Lucyle T. Werkmeister Professor of Philosophy and the Director of the Program in the History and Philosophy of Science at Florida State University. He is Professor Emeritus at the University of Guelph, in Ontario, Canada. He is a former Guggenheim fellow and Gifford lecturer. He is the author or editor of over sixty books, most recently *Darwinism as Religion: What Literature Tells Us about Evolution*; *On Purpose*; *The Problem of War: Darwinism, Christianity, and their Battle to Understand Human Conflict*; and *A Meaning to Life*.

About the Series

This Cambridge Elements series provides concise and structured introductions to all of the central topics in the philosophy of biology. Contributors to the series are cutting-edge researchers who offer balanced, comprehensive coverage of multiple perspectives, while also developing new ideas and arguments from a unique viewpoint.

Cambridge Elements ≡

Philosophy of Biology

Elements in the Series

A full series listing is available at: www.cambridge.org/EPBY